THE MAINSTAY OF AMERICAN INDIVIDUALISM

A Survey of the Farm Question

BY THE SAME AUTHOR

REGULATION OF PUBLIC UTILITIES

A Crucial Problem in Constitutional Government (1932)

THE MAINSTAY
OF
AMERICAN INDIVIDUALISM

A Survey of the Farm Question

BY
CASSIUS M. CLAY

NEW YORK
THE MACMILLAN COMPANY
1934

Set up and printed.
Published February, 1934.

PRINTED IN THE UNITED STATES OF AMERICA
NORWOOD PRESS LINOTYPE, INC.
NORWOOD, MASS., U.S.A.

TO THREE LITTLE BOYS

CASSIUS, LANDON AND HARRIS

One or more of whom may some day
be glad, amid the increasing complexities
of a Machine Age, to seek the contentments
of a farm life

The prosperity of those who till the soil lies at the basis of world prosperity

REPORT OF COUNCIL OF ROYAL INSTITUTE OF INTERNATIONAL AFFAIRS

In my opinion, no great division of human society has ever been lied to, and lied about, as much in the same period of time, as has the American farmer in the last ten years. He has been the victim of more false economic and political information, with its constant destruction of public confidence in everything he is and represents, than has any other element in our social structure

MELVIN A. TAYLOR

Providence takes care of drunks, fools, and the United States of America

OLD ADAGE

PREFACE

ALTHOUGH the author cannot inscribe after his name a degree as an agricultural economist, for nearly ten years he has been conversant with the economic literature evoked by the farm relief controversy. With this background and a dichotomy of cultural environment he combines a profound sympathy with the farming point of view and a conviction that the plight of the farmers generally justifies an honest endeavor to see the woods in spite of the trees.

As far back as the author has any personal knowledge, his family on both sides have depended for their means of livelihood upon farming. Part of this book was written within the quiet of the author's family home, the bricks of which were fashioned in the yard with a hand-mold before the building of a railroad to the local county-seat. In that environment and on a farm which for several generations has been operated as a successful business enterprise, the more impressionable half of his life has been spent.

The remaining half, including ten years of active practise of the legal profession in New York City, has afforded, on the other hand, realistic contacts with the world of industry, transportation and banking. In keeping with this bifurcation of personal experience, part of this book was written in the heart of that great metropolis, within the very shadow of the Empire State Building which, as if in challenge to America's unknown destiny, lifts against "an implacable sky" a gleaming tower that caps a hundred half-vacant floors.

In the following pages, the nexus of forces that hold in their grip the future of two neighborhoods so contrasting and so seemingly remote are analyzed from a distinctly agrarian point of view. Too many books on farm relief appear to the author to view the question through the spectacles of industrialism, or to arrive at conclusions that appeal neither to the farmers themselves nor to the dominant forces in contemporary America.

For such deficiencies as may appear in this volume, the author tenders to the critics, in extenuation, the baffling complexities of the problem and the absolute impossibility that a lay student can explore at all adequately its extremely prolix and controversial ramifications.

The amount of available material—ranging all the way from the solid books by recognized authorities to feature articles and editorials in the daily press—is literally appalling. To buttress his analysis, the author has not hesitated to resort freely to some of the most distinguished of this literature, including what, within the examination permitted by the time at the author's disposal, seemed best among various magazine and newspaper articles. Those familiar with the subject will doubtless recognize various scraps of thought and information taken, without leave for taking, from a multitude of sources.

Grateful acknowledgment is due to Columbia University

Press, Commerce Clearing House, Inc., D. Appleton-Century Company (incorporated), Harcourt, Brace and Company, Inc., Harper & Brothers, Henry Holt and Company, Little, Brown & Company, McGraw-Hill Book Company, Inc., Minton, Balch & Company, The Bobbs-Merrill Company, The Business Bourse, the University of Chicago Press, the University of Wisconsin and William Morrow & Company, Inc., and the publishers of the American Economic Review, Atlantic Monthly, Current History Magazine, Forum Magazine, Harvard Business Review, Journal of Farm Economics, National Sphere, New York Times, Saturday Evening Post, The Nation, The New Republic, World's Work, Yale Review, and of the proceedings of The Academy of Political Science, for their kind coöperation in permitting the use of quotations from various copyrighted books and periodical publications identified in footnotes to the text. The author is likewise under obligations to perhaps half a dozen friends who have been good enough to read the manuscript of this book, either in whole or in part, and give him helpful suggestions. To Professor John D. Black of Harvard, with whom his contact has been entirely by correspondence, he is deeply indebted for valuable technical criticisms of a part of the manuscript.

Most of the book was written before the development of the 1932 political campaign. Parts of several chapters were rewritten and chapter VII added in July, 1933. As kaleidoscopic changes are occurring in the whole picture, no attempt has been made at general revision beyond the latter date. While a life-long Democrat and presenting the traditional Democratic viewpoint on the tariff the author's endeavor throughout has been to explore and to inform rather than to allow his conclusions to be distorted by partisan considerations. His aim has been to relate present difficulties to the flow of past events and thus to provide an integrated viewpoint of the whole subject.

From a personal viewpoint the author's deliberate choice of stressing the underlying policies involved rather than special measures, has the further advantage of avoiding the battle lines of immediate political warfare.

When it is realized that the farm question is a century-old problem that goes to the roots of American life, the reader will comprehend how in a very real sense the farming community is the mainstay of American individualism, the rightful heirs to a historic tradition which continues to command the lip service of those high in the nation's business and political activities.

It might be mentioned that in this volume the writer has authority to speak for no one but himself. In this respect he is faithful to the dominant characteristic of the farmers, whose truly individualistic social attitude is separately a source of strength and collectively a weakness.

C. M. C.

CONTENTS

THE MAINSTAY OF AMERICAN INDIVIDUALISM

A Survey of the Farm Question

CHAPTER I

PERSPECTIVE

A FUNDAMENTAL peculiarity of the agricultural crisis has been its world-wide character. All over the world the producers of food and raw materials have been in difficulties, including the wheat growers of Canada, the United States and the Argentine; the cotton planters of the United States, Egypt and India; the coffee planters of Brazil; the rubber planters of the English possessions and the Dutch East Indies; the producers of camphor and silk in Japan; the sugar planters of Cuba and elsewhere; the sisal planters of the Yucatan; the miners of copper in the United States, of silver in Mexico, of nitrates in Chile; the growers of currants in Greece, of jute in India, of dark tobacco in Kentucky; the producers of wool, cattle and hides in many lands.

The crisis, furthermore, has been the culmination of a period of depression that has lasted over a considerable time.

The measures which various nations have adopted in an attempt to protect their own producers have, almost without exception, disastrously failed. One scarcely need mention the various attempts to exploit the foreign consumer, such as the Stevenson rubber plan, coffee valorization in Brazil, the sisal export tax, the controls of the production of Chilean nitrate, Egyptian cotton, Japanese silk and the like. The fall of copper from twenty-four cents to a recent low of five cents has furnished an example close at hand of the futility of artificial controls when fundamentals are unfavorable. Within the United States the losses of the Federal Farm Board in its "stabilization" operations in wheat and cotton illustrate the hazards of a bold attempt to restrain the free play of economic forces. In the field of international action, the uncertain outcome of the Chadbourne sugar stabilization plan raises anew doubts which were entertained by some at its inception.

A study of the history of measures of this sort discloses that they usually originate in periods of price-decline, when the odds are against success.

Commodity prices all over the world have been in a secular trend downwards since 1920.

Of the causes of this decline there is fairly general agreement among economists. The experts differ profoundly as to the means of overcoming it.

The report of the Economic Committee of the League of Nations, published in 1931, was concurred in by the agricultural section of the Committee and experts in agricultural economy from twenty-four countries, including the United States. This report lists as the principal causes of the international depression in agriculture: changes in consumption; overproduction of certain products due to the "technical progress of agriculture" and economic dislocations caused by the War; monetary fluctuations; monopolies; and protectionism.

At the second International Conference on Agricultural Economics which convened at Cornell University in August, 1930, there assembled agricultural economists, scientists and farm leaders from twenty-one countries. An examination of the proceedings discloses less unanimity than is expressed in the League of Nations report, yet the contours of the discussion confirm in a general way the diagnosis of the latter. The picture that emerges from the deliberations of a world "grotesquely unbalanced in regard to the supply and distribution of necessities" is graphically described by one observer, as follows:

"Figuratively, there are in Australia and in the United States mountains of wool and cotton which people in other parts of the world need; but artificial trade restraints hamper the free exchange of sufficient quantities of wool and cotton. There is a mighty river of wheat flowing from the plains of North America, but the industrial nations of Europe and the hungry millions of China and other parts of the world cannot divert a sufficient part of that stream to themselves because economic and political barriers stop the flow of goods which might be exchanged for wheat. Enormous quantities of butter are produced in the countries of Northern Europe, notably Denmark, but 12,000,000 underfed people in Germany have to eat inferior substitutes because their purchasing power has been destroyed by a combination of political and economic factors which prevents German goods from being directed to places where they are needed. While there is a vast supply of eggs in China, to millions of people in Soviet Russia an egg is a luxury that is reserved for special occasions, such as illness or the great holidays. In Russia there are vast areas rich in things for which the Chinese people hunger, but the land that could banish famine from China lies idle because political factors cut the Soviet Republics off from the huge reservoirs of credit without which the available resources cannot be developed to the fullest extent." [1]

Another fundamental peculiarity of the present agricultural crisis has been that, while it is world-wide in extent, the contributing causes are not necessarily the

[1] Samuel Cahan, *Current History,* October, 1930, p. 77.

same in all countries. This appears from the painstaking and careful analyses of conditions in various countries presented by the scientists at the Cornell Conference; no less so from similar statements annexed as a supplement to the League of Nations report.

In this book we wish to confine our consideration to the causes of, and remedies for, the agricultural depression in the United States. These appear sufficiently specific to permit their being examined without extending the scope of the inquiry to conditions abroad, and thus distracting attention from policies which might alleviate conditions at home.

Nevertheless, since the situation in the United States cannot be separated from the world context, we shall not fatuously attempt so to separate it in the following pages.

The leadership which, without her volition, has been thrust upon America as a result of the World War and which, for better or for worse, she must assume in the years to come requires not only that she set her own house in order but, if for no other reason than that of her own self-interest, that this be done in ways calculated to promote world recovery. Whether he realizes it fully or not, no one has a larger stake in the latter than the American farmer.

As will also appear from the author's thesis, with the farmer, its present mainstay, lies the fate of the creaking system which we venture to dignify as American individualism.

CHAPTER II

CHANGING FRONTIERS

ONE reason for the plight of agriculture in the United States is high costs and low prices.

According to the Department of Agriculture, in January, 1933, the ratio of prices received by farmers to prices paid by farmers was 49 per cent of the corresponding ratio for the five-year period, 1909–1914.

Another reason is debt and taxes.

In 1910 the farm mortgage debt in the United States is estimated to have been $3,320,000,000. In 1932 the total farm indebtedness of all kinds stood at about $12,000,000,000.

From a base level of 100 in 1915, taxes on farm property rose to 265 in 1929. Since 1929 they have fallen about 20 per cent.

These figures are more eloquent than a mass of statistics.

That the economic inequality under which the farmers labor is due to temporary conditions and will tend to disappear with the return of prosperity, is a common fallacy.

As a matter of fact, the roots of the agricultural depression penetrate deeply, as a survey of changing economic frontiers will disclose.

The need of special assistance to the farmers becomes

more clear when we realize that the present crisis results not only from causes which are responsible for the general drop in prices but also from special factors which have over a considerable period of time operated to increase the special hazards characteristic of farming.

In this chapter we shall endeavor to review the more important of agriculture's changing frontiers. It is advisable that first the reader should have before him a picture of the contemporary farm situation, with its constantly varying lights and shades.

Changes in Consumption. These have adversely affected some producers, but (no less importantly) benefited others. A general decline in the *per capita* consumption of principal farm products during the depression, due to the decline in general purchasing power, falls in a class by itself. Among the changes over a period of years which have benefited certain producers may be mentioned: the enormous increase in the use of cigarettes, particularly by women since the War; changes in eating habits, such as the trend toward the greater consumption of citrus fruits, vegetables, dairy products and other specialties. As a rule, producers of burley tobacco and the other products mentioned, especially producers of the latter class close to city markets, have fared best since 1920.

Office workers get less exercise and require a lighter diet than people on farms. There would seem to be a connection between the growth of cities during the last decade and a lessened *per capita* demand for such things as beef (which fell 9 per cent between 1909 and 1924) and flour (which between 1889 and 1929 declined 22 per cent). The demand for vitamins brings profits to the truck-gardener; it hurts the producer of fine beefsteak.

Other changes in consumption put at a disadvantage other kinds of farmers. Changes in women's styles alternately decrease and increase the amount of material required for articles of dress. The introduction of cheap rayon cuts into the demand for cotton and the more expensive silk.

The displacement of the horse and the mule by the automobile, the truck and the tractor, between 1910 and 1925, has destroyed a market for corn, oats and hay, to the estimated extent of 15,000,000 acres.

Bernhard Ostrolenk (from whom the above estimates are borrowed) quotes figures, obtained from the Treasury Department and published in the *Congressional Record,* to show that national prohibition reduced the domestic demand for grains to the extent of 65,000,000 bushels of barley, 33,000,000 bushels of corn and 35,000,000 bushels of hops, in each case a larger quantity than was exported from the United States in the year 1925.[1]

Changes in Population. In keeping with a trend that is observable in most of the countries of Western Europe, for the past decade the birthrate in the United States has been declining, dropping from 24 to 19 per 1000. The rate of decline is much greater in the cities than in the rural districts, from which we may fairly conclude that the causes are social and economic rather than due to any diminution of the vitality of the race. In addition, net immigration to the United States has been reduced almost to nothing by the passage of immigration laws and restrictive administrative rulings. Unless the domestic

[1] Ostrolenk, *The Surplus Farmer,* pp. 18–19. Harper & Brothers (1932).

birthrate rises, or more liberal immigration is allowed, students of the subject believe that by 1960 the population of the United States will be approximately stationary.[2]

It takes an average of three children per family to maintain even a stationary population.

Since the farmers have become accustomed to an increase of population and of domestic demand for farm products increasing at the rate of about 15 per cent per decade, the prospect of a stationary population constitutes not the least formidable of American agriculture's economic frontiers.

While changes in consumption and changes in population are to be reckoned with by anyone who attempts to survey the scene impartially, the author does not, by putting them first, wish to over-emphasize them, compared with other fateful factors. Among these, most observers attach great significance to—

Progress of the Agricultural Revolution. There is some evidence that in many countries agricultural production, particularly of wheat, has taken a spurt because of improved machinery.

The so-called agricultural revolution received its first considerable impetus in the United States before the Civil War. It has developed much more slowly and along different lines from the similar development in industry which began with the inventions of Watt, Hargreaves and Cartwright.

Contrary to the popular belief, the progress made by the American farmer in efficiency, taken in the ag-

[2] Baker, "American Agricultural Policy in Relation to Population Growth," Duddy, *Economic Policy for American Agriculture,* University of Chicago Press (1932), pp. 52–55.

gregate, compares very favorably with the aggregate efficiency of American industry. The data compiled by Dr. E. Dana Durant, of the Department of Commerce, shows that between 1899 and 1925 agricultural output per person increased 47 per cent, exactly the same as the increase in the same period in the output per person in manufacturing. High costs stimulate the use of improved machinery. Between 1899 and 1919 agricultural output per person gained 20 per cent and between 1919 and 1925, 18 per cent.[3] By the use of averages it is estimated that in 1880 a farm worker cultivated 21.6 acres; in 1910, 24.8 acres; and in 1925, 32 acres.[4] In the years 1926–1930 production per worker is figured to have been from a quarter to a third more than in the war period ten years before. These marked gains in farm efficiency are figures for the farm industry as a whole, and in the nature of things have been unequally distributed among individual farmers. While some agricultural economists attempt to separate the agricultural revolution into three different phases, designating them respectively as the hand-power phase, the horse-power phase and the motor-power phase, this arbitrary division is of little practical value. As the man on the farm knows, a large part of farm work will always have to be done by hand. On the most up-to-date farms, hand-power, horse-power and motor-power exist side by side today. In the case of such important crops as cotton and tobacco, hand-power predominates. Although, in the case of cotton, production will be revolutionized soon if we can rely on

[3] Thomas, "Significance of Efficiency of American Industry," *The American Economic Review,* Vol. XVIII, No. 1, supplement (March, 1928), pp. 124–125.

[4] Ostrolenk, *op. cit.,* note 1, p. 59.

the optimistic predictions of those familiar with the progress being made towards the perfection of a serviceable cotton-picking machine, invention can do little for the tobacco grower. The cultivation and marketing of the latter crop requires personal attention and hand-work at every stage, from the preparation and care of the seed bed, on through such essential tasks as hoeing, worming and suckering, to the cutting, stripping and grading of the plant leaves. Because so much of the work necessary in the cultivation and preparation of the crop for market must be done by hand, a single tenant, who enters into a share-arrangement with his landlord, cannot handle very well more than six or eight acres of tobacco. Horses or mules are used to plow and prepare the patch in the spring, to pull the tobacco-setter—a machine which has done away with the back-breaking labor of setting the plants by hand—and to draw the wagons of ripe tobacco to the barns for curing. A motor-truck is hired to haul the stripped and graded leaves to the auction-floor in a neighboring town. All the balance of the work is hand-labor, unavoidably so, because of the nature of the crop. To displace hand labor in the stripping and grading of the cured tobacco according to the length, texture and color of the leaves would require a machine not only with a human hand but likewise a human brain.

In other sorts of farming the invention of labor-saving machinery has revolutionized farm work. Except for the cotton gin, the more important inventions of farm machinery have made their appearance within the life of men still living. The self-reaper, it is true, started a revolution on the land prior to the Civil War, but it was not until the seventies and eighties that a crude machine that merely cut the ripened grain and left it unbound in piles on the ground was superseded by the automatic self-binder. The chilled steel plow was first made available to the farmers at a low cost in 1870. In the era of horse-power, crowding upon one another, came other machines revolutionizing from the bottom the methods of farm-production,—the riding-plow, the corn-planter, the wheat-drill, the disc harrow, the mowing-machine and others too numerous to mention. Within the present generation the gas engine, represented by the tractor and the combine and a multitude of other adaptations, has replaced in the furrow and in the field the horse and the mule, and further revolutionized farm production in ways, the more remote consequences of which it is still difficult to apprehend.

These inventions have profoundly altered the conditions under which the average farmer lives and works. Prior to the agricultural revolution a major characteristic of the average farm unit was its self-sufficiency. In the words of Charles A. and Mary Beard, in *The Rise of American Civilization,* this ideal "was never fully realized, of course, but none the less gave a decided bent to rural life." "The essence of the system," as these authors observe, "like the economy of the middle ages, was production for use rather than for exchange or profit and the psychology of that mode of life inhered in all its transactions." The picture they give is one, the substantial correctness of which may still be vouched for by a few sere and withered persons who delight to recall the farm life of their childhood spent, perhaps, in the ante-bellum South, or in the New England hills, or on the flat plains of Iowa, far removed from the invasion of the railroad locomotive:

"Bread came from the corn and wheat fields; milk, butter, cheese, and meat from the pasture; clothing from the backs of the growing flock; wood from the forest; sugar from the maple grove; and leather from the neighboring tanyard. Horses and oxen raised on the farm furnished the motor power, and a few simple and inexpensive tools made up the mechanical equipment. Of the annual produce, a certain amount was sold to bring in cash for current expenses, including taxes, and some was exchanged at the village store for necessities not made at home." [5]

Today, a major characteristic of the average farm unit is its growing dependence upon a capitalist economy. In other words (we quote Mr. Garet Garrett in the *Saturday Evening Post* of July 18, 1931):

"Farming now is a business, requiring investment, capital and credit. To produce food in the modern way a farmer must consume machinery, gasoline, oil, rubber, chemicals, lumber, a thousand other products of mechanical industry; he cannot stop to make his own clothes and shoes, which, in any case, he has forgotten how to do, and these he must buy; more and more, instead of sustaining himself directly from the soil, he buys his own food from the great industries that finish and process the food we eat. This is because agriculture becomes specialized for purposes of commercial production. One farmer produces only poultry and eggs, another only dairy products, another perishable vegetables to be shipped by the trainload in ice—all these by intensive method; by the extensive method one farmer produces only wheat, another only cotton, and so on. The crop is for money; and with the money each one buys from industry those other things which satisfy his needs and natural wants, including a variety of finished food."

In other words, the progress of the agricultural revolution is forcing the farmer more and more into spe-

[5] Charles A. and Mary Beard, *The Rise of American Civilization*, Vol. II, p. 272. The Macmillan Company (1930 ed.).

cialized production and exchange. But here we run into conditions and paradoxes. Farming, as generations of farmers in America have known it, is more than a business; it is a way of life. In order to conserve the fertility of the soil, the good farmer for years has practised a rotation and diversification of crops. "Diversification," in the words of Herbert Quick, "is but another name for good farming."[6] It makes the farmer's income more nearly constant. It renders him less dependent upon weather and market conditions which control the amount of his return from a single crop. It gives the farmer a twelve-months' occupation. It prevents the exhaustion of the fecundity of his land, the silent but steady wasting away of his business capital. It provides him with production for sustenance, food for his table and supplies for his cellar.

On the other hand, it does not necessarily mean farming for maximum profit. Farming for maximum profit tends to specialized production and exchange. It means, within broad and indefinite limits, special types of farming in special regions. It means the production and sale of those farm products for which a special region, because of natural or artificial advantages, is best adapted; specialization in the kind of farming which is more efficient in that region than in others; as, for instance, hay in New England; dairying, poultry and vegetable enterprises near the great cities; tobacco for cigar-wrappers in the Connecticut valley; flue-cured leaf in the Carolinas, burley and dark tobacco in Kentucky and Tennessee; cotton in the South; corn, cattle and hogs

[6] From *The Real Trouble with the Farmers,* p. 79, by Herbert Quick, copyright 1924, used by special permission of the publishers, The Bobbs-Merrill Company.

in the corn belt; wheat on the great plains; sugar-cane in Louisiana; sugar beets and sheep-herding in the Rocky Mountain states; citrus fruits in California and Florida; apples in Oregon and peaches in Georgia, etc.

In formerly diversified regions the trend is toward less diversification, but not toward complete specialization. For most of the country the trend is toward one major enterprise with minor enterprises supplementary and complementary to it. Only in favored regions, possessing a combination of natural advantages, is this not true. Of these the corn belt is the largest single area of its kind—one of the greatest farming regions in the world. Other instances peculiarly blessed by nature in which general farming flourishes under normal conditions are far-famed: the valley of Pennsylvania, the blue-grass region of Kentucky, parts of Texas and the West.

Specialized production and exchange, so familiar among the big industries, by creating a variety of new goods and increasing the supply available for man's use, have made possible so-called modern standards of living. They have made possible the great volume of modern trade. However much the sentimentalist may deplore the passing of the self-sustaining farm unit of pioneer days, farmers can no more resist the tendency than they can resist economic change. As a business man, the farmer turns to the special type of farming which hard experience, if nothing else, has taught him is most likely, in the region where his farm is located, to bring him the largest cash return.

Each successive improvement in farm machinery accentuates this trend towards a specialized type of farming. The working of this economic principle is especially observable since the introduction of power machinery. The most obvious instance is the case of wheat. It has been estimated that the cost of harvesting and threshing a bushel of wheat with a combine is about seven cents, against about twenty-seven cents by the old method. The combine, however, requires a large initial outlay, and because of depreciation and obsolescence, which run on after the brief wear and tear of the harvest season is over, its use is uneconomic except on large acreages of land. It is particularly suited for use on a particular kind of land—relatively cheap but level land such as is found in the wheat country of the West. The effect of the introduction of power machinery upon the small wheat farmer may be noted in the author's home state which, though a rolling country, contains one of the most fertile farm regions in the United States. Here, twenty years ago, wheat was grown by many of the best farmers as a regular rotation after corn. Because, however, wheat was grown in connection with general farming, it was cultivated in relatively small areas—rarely more than 50 or 75 acres to the field. The land, not being level, is not suited to the most economic use of the combine. Furthermore, due to the exhaustion, through long years of cultivation without fertilizing, of the life-giving lime in the soil, the yield of wheat even on the best land has in recent years become uncertain and erratic. Today, such wheat as is grown in the region frequently does not pay the costs of seed, the labor, and the harvesting and threshing. Relatively little wheat is now grown because few growers can compete successfully year after year with sections which have the advantages of low-priced land and power machinery. For these reasons, rather than because of the collapse in the market price for the grain, the farmer for profit, if he is to realize a fair return on his capital investment in the land, must turn to farm activities which can be put on an economic basis in the region. Because the region is particularly suited to the breeding of fine horses and livestock and the production of tobacco, we have another illustration of the forces which operate for more and more specialized production. It may or may not be specially significant in this connection that in the year 1931, which was an exceptionally good growing year, the production of burley tobacco was estimated by the United States Department of Agriculture as the largest on record, and more than sixty million pounds in excess of the current five-year average. The estimated acreage of burley tobacco for the same period was estimated to have exceeded the five-year average by more than one-fourth.

The progress of the agricultural revolution makes the farmer increasingly dependent upon one or more special cash crops; at the same time he must incur a greater capital outlay for machinery and fertilizers. He must buy more of the general products of industry to keep pace with advances in the general standard of living of other classes of the population. On all sides does he find his "personal fortunes [to use the words of the authors of *The Rise of American Civilization*] like those of manufacturers and capitalists, linked with the caprices and casualties of domestic and foreign trade."[7]

In the struggle for economic survival, the farmer has one important advantage over the white-collar worker in the cities. He need never lack a roof over his head, food

[7] Charles A. and Mary Beard, *op. cit.*, note 5, p. 275.

on his table and a twelve months' job. By farming for sustenance only he can shield himself against too great dependence upon a treacherous capitalist economy, the slings and darts of an economic system that is either unmanageable or has been grossly mismanaged by the industrialist, the financier and the politician. That is, he can do so if he is willing to fall behind in the great American game of trying to keep up with the Joneses.

Being human, few farmers are willing so to fall behind. Professor John D. Black, former chief economist of the Federal Farm Board, points out that the striking rise in farm indebtedness in the past decade may be attributed in some measure to the fact that the farmers, in their endeavor to participate in rising standards of living shared by other groups, have been living in good part on their capital.[8]

Mass-production in industry, while it has cheapened the cost of many manufactured goods, has multiplied the range and variety of things which can be purchased. Articles once regarded as luxuries have come to be accepted as necessaries in the so-called American standard of living. The farmer who farms principally for sustenance must, figuratively speaking, use his Model T Ford until it wears out. Instead of Hart, Schaffner & Marx clothes, he must continue to get his overalls at the village store and pay for them in eggs and surplus milk. He cannot, to any great extent, go in for super-heterodyne radio sets and electric refrigerators. He must follow the philosophical advice of Sydney Smith: "If you want to make much of a small income, always ask yourself two ques-

[8] Black, *Agricultural Reform in the United States,* p. 36. McGraw-Hill Book Company (1929).

tions: First, do I want it? secondly, can I do without it? These two questions, answered honestly, will double your income."

This policy, based as it is on resistance to the tide of economic change, is not calculated to arouse any enthusiasm among farm leaders. It is, however, one that many small farmers, in a decade of high costs and low prices, have, either from necessity or shrewd native intelligence, accepted. How far the farmers, as a group, are behind other groups in the struggle with rising standards of living may be gauged by comparing the figures as to such elementary matters as health facilities and mechanical conveniences. A report published in the 1926 Yearbook of the Department of Agriculture, representing three thousand homes in eleven widely separated states, is illuminating in the absence of more comprehensive data:

> "Slightly more than one-twentieth, or 5.7 per cent., of the homes were completely modern, that is, fitted with central heating and central lighting systems, running water, kitchen sink, bath-room (equipped with stationary tub and bowl), indoor toilet and sewerage disposal. About one-fifth, or 20.8 per cent., of the homes were fitted with a part of the improvements named, and almost three-fourths, 73.5 per cent., of the homes lacked all modern improvements."

Against the disadvantages of fewer modern conveniences, fewer good schools, doctors, hospitals and the like, the farmer must balance better air, more sunlight and less noise.

The progress of the agricultural revolution and the increasing use of farm machinery has made the economic position of the quarter-section wheat farmer particularly precarious. Since 1920 the number of tractors on farms in the United States has grown from 246,000 to over 900,000. According to Secretary Hyde in the 1931 annual report of the Department of Agriculture, there were 84,000 fewer farms in 1930 than in 1925, but there were 15,000,000 more acres in crops. The extent to which mechanical energy is replacing horse-power is shown by the decrease in the number of horses on farms from 19,767,161 in 1920 to 13,383,574 in 1930; of the number of mules from 5,432,391 to 5,353,993.

The small wheat grower is faced with the alternative, either of going out of business or of substituting for wheat-growing, dairying or something else that will afford a fair living on a quarter-section farm. Unless he chooses the latter alternative he is in grave danger of being squeezed out by the march of the combine on the great plains. According to Martel P. McNeely, in *The Country Gentleman* for July, 1931, the smallest grain farm that could keep the smallest unit of the new machinery busy enough for attractive profits is 1,000 to 1,200 acres. In the Texas panhandle north of Amarillo there was a field in 1931 of more than 30,000 acres. It is estimated that there are twenty to twenty-five thousand combines in the State of Kansas alone. Over the long-term, little that the government can do to raise the price of wheat by artificial means will help the plight of the small grower, for raising the price of wheat will encourage capital to go into wheat ranching. The McNary-Haugen plan, the export debenture, to the extent that they can be made successful, would have the same effect. Thomas D. Campbell has farmed a 95,000 acre wheat ranch in Montana and was financed for a time by J. P. Morgan & Co. Hickman Price, who three or four years ago gave up a $50,000 per year job with the Fox Film Company to become Texas' largest wheat farmer, by intensive cultivation and the proper use of mechanical equipment, grew wheat at a true cost of forty cents per bushel, or less, according to land and season. Kansas legislators may fulminate against corporation farming, but in that state the Sledd Farm Corporation, according to its Vice-President, C. E. Norduff, has been able to produce wheat at a cost of twenty-six cents per bushel. With private capital, these and others have been doing, on the great American plains, what the Soviet government is attempting to do on the vast state farms in Russia. Legislation to restrict corporate or large-scale wheat farming in the United States will not stop it in other lands and in other nations. It may handicap America's power to compete in the world markets.

Combine wheat farming not only tends to glut the world markets with cheap wheat but, by displacing horse- and mule-power on the farms, diverts land heretofore used for the growing of corn, oats and hay to the production of human food.

Savants, faced with the alarming situation of the small wheat grower and seeking to trace the portents in the sky, see in his predicament the fate of the general run of small farmers. We wonder. Farming is an occupation of a thousand contrasts. The farmers, as a group, have shown great adaptability to economic change in the past. Such types of farming as animal production, tobacco-growing, dairy and vegetable enterprises, fruit culture, and others too numerous to mention, do not necessarily increase in efficiency with size. The best beef-cattle are produced on the general farm. The great herds of Texas longhorns passed with the passing of the cowboy. The growing of cotton, which was revolutionized by the invention of the cotton gin, is still carried on by tenant negro farmers; and to anyone familiar with the South it is difficult to conceive that this system can be entirely displaced, whatever further revolution the coming of a mechanical cotton-picker may bring to the Cotton Kingdom.

Without question, the small wheat farmer can dig in against the assimilation of his business into a capitalist economy by farming for sustenance and contenting himself with a fair living. He might suffer a worse fate. It is better than giving up his job and hiking to the city to swell the bread-lines which threaten to continue to characterize the Age of the Machine, even after the return of prosperity.

For the time being, strange to say, the wheat-grower on a moderate-sized farm is standing up in the depression better than the big fellows who are heels over head in debt on land bought at high prices for motorized production. From the West filter stories that some of the latter are flat on their backs because of an inability to meet payments on debt-encumbered lands, the value of which has been swept away by the economic blizzard.

Changes in consumption affect industry as well as farming. To illustrate this statement one needs only to mention how the coming of the automobile destroyed fortunes which were invested in the manufacture of buggies. The invention of machinery for factory use ushered in the industrial revolution before the use of improved machinery in farming provided the stimulus for a revolution on the land. Changes such as these, while in the last analysis due to man-made forces, must be regarded as essentially economic. They are going on all the time. There is little that one can do to retard their inevitableness. They are at work in industry as well as agriculture. While they make for business instability, they are the price of progress.

The changing frontiers to which the balance of this chapter will be devoted cannot be so simply characterized. They will be discussed under the headings, (1) the decline of competition, (2) the rise in federal, state and local taxation, and (3) lowered foreign demand.

Economists no doubt will question the sufficiency of these headings. Needless to say, the risks of error are large in any analysis which attempts to segregate the elements in a situation so complex as the farm problem.

While agricultural experts recognize numerous other factors in the present crisis and differ among themselves in the emphasis to be placed on each, few will dispute the relevance of the following.

1. *The Decline of Competition.* According to the economics taught in the schools, prices of things are determined by the supply and the demand.

Most authorities recognize that this elementary principle is subject to qualifications; that what the economists refer to as the price-system has become decrepit. A part of the price-system no longer responds quickly to changes in supply and demand. We have, in other words, a situation of half-competition and half-monopoly. While the farmers, when they sell, compete with each other and with the farmers of other nations, other industries and groups sell on a restricted market.

The cruel injustice of this to the farmer appears most

clearly in a period of deflation. The present agricultural crisis is due in no small degree to the effects of the inflation and deflation which have followed the World War, combined with the growing inelasticity of the price-system and the inelasticity of such matters as debt and taxes.

The economic dislocations during the War created an abnormal demand for American farm products. Whatever gains the farmers received in the period of inflation during and just after the period of the War have been wiped out in the succeeding deflation.

Agriculture has borne the greater share of the deflation because in many essentials it is unlike other industries. In the words of Professor E. R. A. Seligman, of Columbia University:

> "The farm price is a wholesale price, not a retail price; it is a producer's price and not a consumer's price; it is the price of a raw material and not of a finished product; it is a price of vegetable and animal products and not of forest and mineral products."[9]

While in a period of falling prices industries suffer generally, the prices of farm and other raw products fall first, fastest and farthest for a variety of reasons.

Because the farmer must plan his production a year in advance (longer in the case of stock-breeding), he cannot as readily as other industries plan production to suit changes in demand. The size of his annual crop depends less upon the acreage than upon the vagaries of weather and rainfall. His expenses in connection with his farm are largely fixed charges—interest on his investment in

[9] Reprinted from Seligman, *The Economics of Farm Relief* (1929), p. 58 with the permission of Columbia University Press.

land, taxes, wages, etc., from which there is no way of relief. These go on, irrespective of the price of his crop or the volume of his production. Again, the price of what he has to sell is determined in competitive markets. Farm staples, such as cotton, wheat and tobacco, sell on an export basis. The price the farmer receives is ordinarily a world price. The price of other staples, such as corn, of which we export a smaller quantity, nevertheless tends to follow the price of other grains. One reason is fairly clear. When, as in 1930, there is a big wheat crop and a shortage of corn, some farmers sell corn and feed wheat to their stock.

When prices fall, the only way an individual farmer can show a profit over fixed charges is by increasing his yield. To keep away the sheriff, he has to produce more.

Because people do not necessarily eat more food when prices are low, this increased production meets an inelastic demand. It has been figured that the average American consumes annually 110 pounds of sugar, 3.5 bushels of potatoes and 4.5 bushels of wheat. Regardless of price, these figures seldom vary by as much as 15 per cent.[10]

Deflation catches the farmers in a vicious circle. The single farmer reacts to falling prices by increasing output. He has to because, individually, he is better off with a big crop, even at a low price. The individual reaction enlarges the aggregate production, thus increasing the market supply and causing the downward trend of prices to continue. Efficiency in production, while enabling the individual to meet rigid costs, aggravates the situation of the farmers as a group.

[10] Wiley, *Agriculture and the Business Cycle since 1920*, p. 58, University of Wisconsin (1930).

The cheapening of prices would not result in hardship if all prices declined together and in the same proportion. If the price-system were completely elastic and all prices, together with fixed charges such as interest, taxes and wages, rose or fell together, no one would be made poorer by a general drop in prices, provided he was out of debt. But to the extent that the price-system has become rigid, prices do not decline together and in the same proportion. The unevenness of the decline tends to enrich certain groups at the expense of others.

Only certain kinds of farmers, in certain sections, participated in any appreciable degree in America's golden era of bootstrap prosperity that ended in 1929. From 1920 to the end of 1924, and in a lesser degree until 1929, there was a continuous disparity between the price of the things the farmer sells and the price of the things he buys.

Because the price of farm staples, which are on an export basis, are ordinarily determined on world markets, this economic inequality tends to be intensely aggravated when a general drop in prices occurs. The collapse in 1920–1921 of the inflated price levels of the War period was even sharper than has been the collapse of farm prices since 1929. Chicago wheat fell from $3.10 per bushel in May, 1920, to almost $1 in November, 1921; Chicago corn from $2.10 per bushel in August, 1919, to 42 cents per bushel in October, 1921; wool from 50 cents per pound in the first part of 1920, to 20 cents before the end of 1921; and sheep from $10.66 in primary markets in April, 1920, to $5.11 a year later.[11]

What has happened since 1929 is only too well known to the farmers to whom it has brought ruin. The mount-

[11] Wiley, *op. cit.*, note 10, p. 14.

ing crop of impaired reserves, omitted dividends and insolvencies in other industries, should not obscure the significant facts worked out for the National Bureau of Economic Research by Dr. Frederick C. Mills with respect to the course of prices between July, 1929, and October, 1931. This study discloses that between these dates the purchasing power of raw materials had *decreased* 13.4 per cent per unit, that of raw farm products 24.8 per cent, while real prices, or the purchasing power per unit of manufactured goods, had *increased* 6.1 per cent.[12]

A reason why agriculture suffers more severely than other industries in a general drop of prices is that the ability to limit competition has not been developed in agriculture as in other industries. As we have already mentioned, the individual farmer, in order to meet items in the nature of fixed charges, reacts to falling prices by producing more. Furthermore, it is not at all certain that agriculture would benefit from curtailing its production in depressions.

Industry, on the other hand, reacts to falling prices by restricting production in an endeavor to maintain prices. It can do this because of (1) inherent differences between farming and manufacturing and (2) the decline in competition in manufacturing, which gives a greater control over production.

The primary concern of both the farmer and the manufacturer is of course the same—profits. The effort of the one to make a profit by increasing his efficiency in production and of the other to do so by cutting output to maintain prices, both tend to widen the disparity between

[12] Cited in an editorial in *The New Republic,* Jan. 27, 1932, p. 282.

agricultural and non-agricultural prices when prices begin to drop generally.

From the different ways in which the farmer and the manufacturer react to falling prices, one should not imply that the farmer is less shrewd or less capable as a business man than the latter. The manufacturer's method of meeting a depression is not necessarily productive of profits, as mounting deficits and insolvencies in industry tellingly illustrate. It does mean that because of the increasing concentration of control in manufacturing, the industrialist is able to exert control over output.

While the urgency which compels the farmer to produce more tends to aggravate the price decline, the manufacturer's attempt to stabilize prices by restricting output likewise tends to postpone and aggravate the liquidating process. Manufacturing prices come down, but they come down more slowly and not so far as agricultural prices. The endeavor to maintain prices by cutting output, such as is practised in the steel and most other mass-production industries, throws thousands out of work.

While people still have to eat, unemployment sharply reduces the normal demand for the more expensive articles of diet. For beef and mutton, cheaper foods are substituted such as potatoes and other starches. The slowing down of manufacturing production creates a surplus of agricultural products, such as cotton and hides, used in industry. All groups suffer, but all do not suffer in the same degree.

The manufacturer and the owners of the plant suffer because profits disappear.

Labor suffers more acutely because it is dependent on the weekly pay-envelope. When the plant closes down, it cannot live on its reserves, as can the owners of the plant.

The farmer suffers because much of the difficulty is passed back to the producer of raw materials. Both the plant and the men who formerly worked in it are consumers of farm products. The plant and the men both remain idle until stocks on hand and in the channels of trade are disposed of and new orders appear.

The plant does not reopen until the products of the plant are wanted badly enough so that they will sell at a price somewhere near the price that existed before the plant closed.

The farmer cannot cut down his costs by throwing people out of work. As the United States Census figures show, over two-thirds of all people gainfully employed on farms are either owners, managers or tenants. Unlike the manufacturer, the farmer's struggle for survival involves enlarged production through improved efficiency. The benefits of this improved efficiency are passed on to the other groups in cheap foods and raw materials.

Why improved efficiency in manufacturing is not equally shared constitutes one of the challenges of the age. No fair-minded person would dispute that the public has been a large gainer from standardized production of a vast array of articles which modern industry has made available at lower prices than would have been deemed possible a generation ago. Yet in spite of this, such problems as industrial unemployment and the disparity between the manufacturers' prices and farm prices show that, in spite of the advances made, the problem of how these benefits may be more equally distributed remains far from solution.

At the present time the farmer has a less strategic

position than any other group. He is in a less strategic position than the laborer who belongs to one of the powerful unions. He is in a less strategic position than the manufacturer. Over a large part of industry, especially that in which economies can be effected through mass-production methods, the size of the companies has become very great.

Consequently, in these fields the characteristics of partial monopoly prevail. Dr. Harry W. Laidler, President of the Bureau of Economic Research, lists the following instances in which corporations whose names have become household bywords dominate the field:

"One corporation—the International Harvester Company—manufactures about half of the farm-machinery of the country. One corporation—the Aluminum Company of America—does a good share of our aluminum business and owns over nine-tenths of the bauxite deposits, from which aluminum is made. One corporation has a practical monopoly of sleeping and parlor-car service. One corporation manufactures a vast majority of cash registers.

"Two corporations—the Ford and the General Motors—turned out three out of every four cars produced in 1930. Two corporations control over fifty per cent. of the country's steel capacity. Two corporations—the General Electric and the Westinghouse—are responsible for most of our electrical machinery. Two others divide between them the making of the country's locomotives. Two dominate the manufacture of passenger and freight trains. Two handle some fifty per cent. of the meat entering into interstate commerce. Two manufactured in 1930 two out of every three cigarettes sold." [13]

The managerial or financial geniuses that control these huge units may possess less than the amount of greed possessed by the average human being, but in combination

[13] Laidler, in *The Federal Anti-trust Laws, A Symposium,* p. 167. Commerce Clearing House, Inc. (1932).

with their unexampled economic power, they possess a balance which is not always sincerely weighted for the greatest public good.

At the present time the old cry against the trusts has subsided, and the general public appears to have accepted big business as an integral part of the economic structure of the country, necessary if America is to continue to compete in the markets of the world with the cartels and trusts of other nations.

However, several consequences follow from a situation of half-competition and half-monopoly. Combinations in industry, by their size and their association with each other, are able to maintain the prices of manufactured products at a sacrifice of the volume of sales. While in a general drop in prices restriction of output may restrict losses, it does not necessarily produce profits. Instead of stabilizing economic conditions, cutting industrial output results in industrial unemployment and a generally lowered standard of living all around, without necessarily producing profits for the big industries. Cutting industrial output and increasing agricultural output tends to widen the disparity between the purchasing power of industry and other groups.

Industrial mergers and the practice of big business in cutting output, which, after all, is merely following the dictates of intelligent self-interest, are not, of course, the only factors in the decline of competition. The rigidity of prices other than farm prices may be ascribed variously to the tariff, a rigid system of transportation rates, the power exerted by the labor unions over wage-levels, the prevalence of price-restrictions and concerted action to maintain prices in various trades, maintenance of manufacturers' retail prices, the international gold situation and the inelasticity of credits generally. All these factors undoubtedly figure in the situation and dovetail into one another. We cannot here go deeply into the subject, especially since the rôle played in the situation by the tariff and various of the factors which we have mentioned will be discussed more fully in succeeding pages. Those best informed on the subject do not need to be told that, in a machine age such as the present, agriculture calls for special consideration at the hands of the government.

Particularly does this need appear during a drastic deflation of prices. Senator Arthur Capper, in his book entitled *The Agricultural Bloc,* figured out the purchasing power of a bushel of wheat during the years 1919–1921, in terms of certain other commodities. According to his computations, which were based on farm prices, 1 bushel of corn in 1919 bought 5 gallons of gasoline; in 1920, 1 gallon; and in 1921 only ½ gallon. While in 1919 a ton of coal cost 6 bushels of corn; in 1920 it cost 40 bushels; and in 1921, 60 bushels. A suit of clothes in 1919 cost 40 bushels; in 1920, 200 bushels; and in 1921, 300 bushels.[14]

The farmers are in a desperate plight today because of a comparable situation. Charles Merz, writing in the *New York Times* of May 15, 1932, quotes figures showing that the declines in prices of different commodities have been far more unevenly distributed than in 1920–1921. Although the value of farm products (measured in terms of the Bureau of Labor Statistics index) had fallen 52.9 per cent since July, 1929, the value of farm imple-

[14] Capper, *The Agriculture Bloc,* p. 38.

ments had fallen only 13.4 per cent. Although hides and leather had fallen 31.6 per cent, boots and shoes were within 16.6 per cent of their 1929 level. Lumber had dropped 29.5 per cent and bricks only 11.1.

Lest the reader may question the soundness of the emphasis that the author has attached to the decline in competition and the rigidity of certain prices, it may be well to mention the star example of cigarette tobacco. Although the grower received for his 1931 crop only about half as much per pound as he did for the 1930 crop, during 1931 at least two of the large tobacco companies were able to move against the tide and report larger net earnings than in 1930. They were able to do this partly because the price of cigarettes was raised in 1931.[15]

[15] *Cf.* the following from a press release of the Agricultural Adjustment Administration of the United States Department of Agriculture, dated September 22, 1933:

"In 1923 the combined total of the amount paid to tobacco growers for all tobacco retained for use in the United States and the net profits of manufacturers was approximately two hundred and fifty million ($250,000,000) dollars. Of this amount one hundred and seventy-four million ($174,000,000) dollars, or 70 per cent, was received by tobacco growers and seventy-six million ($76,000,000) dollars, or 30 per cent, was manufacturers' profits. Since that time the profits of manufacturers have increased steadily and the amount paid to farmers has declined. This decline has been particularly great during the past four years. In 1931, the combined total of these two items was two hundred and forty-three million ($243,000,000) dollars, of which tobacco growers received ninety-six million ($96,000,000) dollars, or 40 per cent, and manufacturers' profits were one hundred and forty-seven million ($147,-000,000) dollars, or 60 per cent. In 1932, manufacturers were able to maintain their profits but farmers' receipts were greatly reduced. Of the combined total of these two items in 1932, which was two hundred and fourteen million ($214,000,000) dollars, the amount received by tobacco growers was only sixty-eight million ($68,000,000) dollars or 32 per cent, and manufacturers' profits were one hundred forty-six millions ($146,000,000) dollars, or 68 per cent. . . .

"In considering the figures just cited it should be pointed out that manufacturers' profits for the most part represent only returns for the capital invested, whereas the amount received by farmers represents the returns for capital, labor and management. Preliminary studies in-

There are at least two opposing schools of thought as to what the farmers can do to raise the purchasing power of farm products and mitigate the severity of future

dicate that the original investment in tobacco manufacturing plants is somewhat less than the original investment in the land, buildings and equipment used in growing the tobacco. In producing the tobacco used by manufacturers last year approximately two hundred and fifty million hours of farm labor were used. If the rate of compensation for this labor were figured at a rate no higher than that paid to the lowest priced labor used by the manufacturer the total returns received by farmers would hardly be sufficient to cover the labor and cash outlays for fertilizers, allowing no return for the capital invested nor compensation for the farmers' management and other miscellaneous items."

The following table is taken from the same press release:

"RELATION BETWEEN GROSS RETURNS TO FARMERS FOR TOBACCO RETAINED FOR DOMESTIC MANUFACTURE AND PROFITS OF 34 LEADING MANUFACTURERS

YEAR	GROSS RECEIPTS OF FARMERS FOR TOBACCO RETAINED FOR DOMESTIC MANUFACTURE	PROFITS OF 34 LEADING DOMESTIC MANUFACTURERS	TOTAL OF FARMERS' RECEIPTS AND MANUFACTURERS' PROFITS	PERCENTAGE DISTRIBUTION	
				Gross Receipts of Farmers	Profits of Manufactures
	Million Dollars	*Million Dollars*	*Million Dollars*	*Per Cent*	*Per cent*
1923	174	76	250	70	30
1924	154	82	236	65	35
1925	141	100	241	59	41
1926	138	104	242	57	43
1927	149	115	264	56	44
1928	161	121	282	57	43
1929	174	134	308	56	44
1930	136	145	281	48	52
1931	96	147	243	40	60
1932	68	146	214	32	68 "

Outside of some newspapers in the tobacco-growing district, these statements have received little notice in the press. They were largely ignored in the metropolitan dailies. Are we to assume that the latter are more susceptible to loss of cigarette advertising, for which one large tobacco company is said to have expended about $20,000,000 in 1931, and another $16,000,000?

price-drops. One school, which is inclined to gloss over the fact that farming is in fundamental ways unlike other industries, takes the view that the cure lies in following the example of industry and labor, which stay the severity of price-declines by maintaining prices and, if necessary to prevent a glut of the market, by restricting output. According to those of this persuasion, the present agricultural crisis is due, in no small degree, to the lack of organization among the farmers.

Another school is still old-fashioned enough to believe that ways can be found to bring about more competition among those with whom the farmers exchange their products. If eventually we eliminate competition throughout the economic order, substituting therefor planned production, it will be necessary to revise the existing basis of American institutions. Property rights will have to be substantially curtailed, since, for reasons which will appear in later pages, it is doubtful whether any scheme which includes as a part of it restriction of agricultural output can be made effective in the long run without governmental coercion of the farmers. Further, it is extremely doubtful if wide-scale planned production, assuming that brains can be found capable of directing the planning wisely and well, is feasible without a revision of the Federal Constitution.

More fundamental considerations are at stake than merely the lack of organization among the farmers. It is obvious also that the agricultural crisis is due to a variety of causes. Decline of competition among those with whom the farmers deal is one of them. Organization of the farmers so as to maintain farm prices and restrict production as industry is able to do, might have mitigated the fall of farm prices; but it is extremely doubtful that its lack is the cause of the present situation. Lack of organization did not prevent farm prices from soaring during and just after the War. As a careful student of the agricultural situation sagely observes: "Lack of organization among farmers cannot play successively the triple rôle of causing normal pre-war prices, fancy war-time prices and wretched bankrupting post-war prices." [16]

2. *The Rise in Federal, State and Local Taxation.* Another cause of the farmer's acute distress is the rise, which has been steadily upward until recently, in federal, state and local taxation.

Under taxation we must include not only visible taxes which the farmer pays to the government, and which he feels when he pays them, but also invisible taxes which are shifted upon him by other groups, and which he pays without realizing that he is paying them. The farmer pays taxes of the latter kind when he buys goods on which a tariff duty has been levied, or goods or services to the price of which a manufacturer or corporation has added an extra charge to cover the latter's tax liability.

Except for the tax on incomes, the way for which was made clear by the income tax amendment to the Constitution, taxes paid to the federal government are of the indirect variety. Since only a small percentage of the total number of farmers in the country have net incomes in excess of the exemption per year (in 1929 the percentage was 13 per cent or 800,000 of the total number of farmers) the farmers have not become aroused over the increase in federal expenditures as they have over the rising burden of direct taxes imposed by state and local authorities.

Between 1913 and 1932, federal expenditures multi-

[16] Wiley, *op. cit.*, note 10, pp. 32–33.

plied over six times, from $724,000,000 to $4,594,000,000, for the fiscal year ended June 30, 1932. In 1932 the expenditures on veterans' relief alone amounted to more than the entire federal budget in 1913.

There is no question that the farmers absorb a much greater share of the burden of federal taxation than they realize. Some economists believe that the overwhelming burden of public debt piled up in many countries during the War has been a principal factor in the world-wide decline of commodity and raw material prices. For this they advance various sound arguments, only one of which we shall mention here.

War, with the inevitable deflation that succeeds it, falls hardest upon agricultural and other raw producers because increased taxation, which follows in the train of war, tends to be shifted to the agricultural or raw producer, both in the form of lower prices for what the agricultural or raw producer has to sell, and higher prices for what he has to buy.

This may not sound simple, but the way it works out is simpler than it appears. It is due to what is known as the incidence of taxation. Behind what is termed the incidence of taxation is the inescapable human equation. No one likes to pay taxes if he can help it. Intelligent self-interest prompts every business man to pass the tax on to someone else if he can, either by subtracting the tax from the price of what he pays for raw materials used in the business, or else by adding the tax, or a large part of it, to the price to the consumer of the finished product.

The ability with which taxes can be shifted varies widely with different groups. The extent of the ability depends upon a number of factors. Taxes are most easily shifted in the case of monopoly. They are least easily shifted in the case of goods sold in a competitive market. We can see how this works by taking an industry, like tobacco manufacturing, which has various monopoly aspects. At the present time the federal government levies an indirect tax of approximately one dollar a pound on certain types of cigarette tobacco.[17] In spite of this exorbitant tax, the tobacco manufacturers who pay this tax to the government are able to make big profits because they shift the tax in part on the grower to whom consequently they pay a lower price for his crop (for the 1931 crop the grower of burley tobacco received on an average less than ten cents a pound), and in part on the consumer of tobacco who, likewise in consequence of the tax, pays more for cigarettes.[18]

Taxes can be shifted if they increase the price which the consumer pays for a product, or in a reverse way they lower the price which a manufacturer pays for raw or unfinished goods. It doesn't depend on the kind of tax, for almost every kind of tax, direct or indirect, can be shifted, except individual income taxes and inheritance taxes. It does depend on the kind of the product and the nature of the market demand. One should not imply that all big industries shift taxes, or that in a multitude of instances it is good business to attempt to do so. If including the tax in the price to the consumer raises the latter price to such extent that the volume of sales is

[17] 1,000 pounds of leaf tobacco per acre is not an unusual average, and the best burley tobacco land will in a good season grow as much as 1500 pounds of leaf tobacco an acre. The federal tax can thus easily amount to more than $1000 per acre.

[18] *Cf.*, note 15.

affected, the manufacturer may find that it is good business not to shift the tax. Similarly, it is not practicable to shift the tax to other shoulders unless competitors do likewise. If including the tax in the price to the consumer cuts down volume of sales, a company, even in a monopoly position, may find it more profitable to pay the tax and recoup itself through the greater profit to be realized from a larger number of sales at a smaller profit per unit. This would seem to be true in some mass-production industries. So keen is competition among the manufacturers of cheap motor cars that one manufacturer cannot raise retail prices without being undersold by other makers.

Only a moment's reflection is required to show that farm operators and tenant farmers are perhaps in a less strategic position than any other group when it comes to shifting taxes. They are producers rather than makers of finished goods. Their income is derived from the sale of animal and vegetable products which are sold on highly competitive markets. Except as consumers, they buy few things other than labor and machinery. When industry is prosperous, they cannot compete with the wages paid in urban communities, and there is a scarcity of farm labor. Machinery is bought from one of the large farm-implement manufacturers at a list price.

The farmer can rarely pass his tax on to others. He usually finds himself as one to whom the tax is shifted.[19]

No group, perhaps, at bottom, is a greater sufferer from the heavy burden of federal expenditures. No group,

[19] *Cf.* Coombs, *Taxation of Farm Property.* U. S. Dept. of Agric. Tech. Bull. No. 172 (1930), p. 4.

perhaps, is a greater loser from war and governmental extravagance.

In the United States we have a triple tax system. While for a generation the costs of the federal government were mounting, they did not mount as high or as steadily as the costs of state and local governments.

Of the entire cost of government in the United States, which is estimated to have mounted from $3,000,000,000 in 1913 to $15,000,000,000 in 1932, the cost of state and local governments constitutes between two-thirds and three-fourths.

As with federal taxation, the farmers suffer from this burden in two ways. Before discussing the critical situation with respect to direct taxation of farm property, a few words will be devoted to the substantial burden of state and local taxation which falls on the farmer in invisible ways, such as in the form of higher retail prices, distribution costs, freight and electric power rates.

Unlike taxes on farm property, taxes on business property in crowded cities are to a considerable extent passed on to tenants and consumers. High taxes on business property tend to be reflected in high rental values, which work into industrial costs in general and, of no less importance to the general public, explain in part the inflexibility of middlemen's charges.

High taxes on public utility properties are shifted in the form of high freight rates and public utility charges.

High taxes, of course, are but a single element in a complex situation which results in the relative inelasticity of middlemen's charges, freight and public utility rates.

One reason is that the groups that dominate these phases of our economic life occupy a strategic position in the channels of trade and public marts, and hence are able to shift the burden of fixed charges of various sorts to the raw producers and general consumers.

Another reason is the dependence of an industrialized society upon credits and borrowed money. During a drastic fall in prices, interest is a fixed charge that can be cut down only by agreement between the debtor and creditor, or through the bankruptcy court.

Another reason is the rigidity of wage-levels. Parallel with the concentration of control in American business and finance, labor, prompted by no less intelligent self-interest, has learned to combine and, through the mechanism of nation-wide unions, to exert a power scarcely less inferior than that of the industrialist and the financier in the changing panorama of national politics.

An important benefit to be derived from the depression is the bitter-sweet realization on the part of the legislative assemblies and public officials that there is a day of reckoning for extravagant public expenditures. The worst offenders have been the municipal authorities. The dire distress of city government in the three largest cities of the nation—New York, Chicago and Philadelphia—distracts attention from similar conditions that prevail in many smaller cities all over the land.

Because high taxes in crowded cities tend to be shifted at least in part to those who live in the country, it is a fallacy to assume that the farmers do not suffer in the long run from wasteful and frenzied municipal spending.

There is another way in which the farmers lose. To the extent that taxes are shifted not to the country, but to the general consuming public in cities, or bear directly upon home-owners in the cities, buying power is lessened and the demand in the city for the products of the farm diminished.

As regards direct taxation of farm property, the situation is no less menacing because it has been well advertised. In many sections farmers are not realizing enough return from their crops to meet the amounts they are called upon to pay to state and local authorities in the form of direct taxes on farm property. In widely scattered states many are abandoning their farms to the sheriff rather than attempt the hopeless task of paying their taxes. Other communities are striking back in angry fashion against the public authorities. The prevailing mood is one of blind resentment against the high costs of local government and those responsible for it.

Mark Sullivan, in the *New York Herald-Tribune* of March 27, 1932, tells of a taxpayer who has put in pungent phrase the way many farmers are reacting to the situation. Having in mind the pink marble edifices in the state capitals and county seats, this countryman exploded: "They build themselves Greek palaces in which to carry on their petty functions, while they leave to the farmer not enough money to paint his house or his barn."

The facts in the situation are easily accessible if not generally known. According to the data compiled by Dr. L. C. Gray, economist in charge of Land Economics in the United States Bureau of Agricultural Economics, taxes on farm property rose between 1915 and 1929 from a base level of 100 to 265. In other words, although the Department of Agriculture reported that farm commodity prices by February, 1933 were only 49 per cent of the five year average of 1909–1914, taxes on farm property were from two to two and one-third times as high as in 1915. In spite of the long depression in farm commodity prices during the last decade, taxes on farm property increased to 265 in 1929 from a level of 163 in 1920.[20]

More arresting than these statistics are the stories that come from various agricultural regions. Newspaper reports that about 25 per cent of the privately owned property in the state of Mississippi was under sale in 1932 for delinquent taxes are matched with accounts of similar trouble in Alabama. The absolute necessity of relief for the owners of real property in those states was the impetus for the enactment of a sales tax in Mississippi and for the drive for a state income tax in Alabama. In Michigan we learn that approximately one-third of the area of the entire state was tax-delinquent at the beginning of 1932. An area equivalent to the remaining two-thirds of the state of Michigan was tax-delinquent in the four states of Wisconsin, Minnesota, South Dakota and Oregon. These are a few samples.

In some states the difficulty arises from the fact that while tax rates were not increased, assessments were increased from fifty to one hundred per cent or more with the inflation of land values soon after the War and have not been sufficiently lowered since. In other states assessed values were not increased so greatly, but tax rates were doubled. In still other states both assessed values and tax rates remain at a high level.

Needless to say, whether his assessment is high and his

[20] Gray, "Overproduction and Agricultural Depression," *Pro. Acad. Pol. Sci.*, Vol. XIV, No. 3, *Depression and Revival* (June, 1931), pp. 48 *ff.*

tax rate low, or his assessment low and his tax rate high, makes little difference to the harassed farmer. In either situation, what matters is the total amount of the tax in relation to his land income.

In all states, but particularly in those in which state and local authorities borrowed heavily through the sale of public bonds, taxpayers face one problem in common. When the purchasing value of the dollar falls, the face amount of the public debt which does not change becomes so much the harder to pay off.

As we shall recur to the problem of taxation in subsequent chapters, we shall content ourselves here with a few obvious observations.

Were public authorities superior to political influences and gifted with economic intelligence greater than that possessed by the average business man, the time to borrow money for public expenditures is when the price of things is near the bottom, instead of when they are at boom levels. In 1927 it took about $1.50 to purchase goods and services which could have been bought for $1.00 in 1914, and for very little more at the present writing. The matter is put in these words by Dr. Coombs in his study of the situation to which we have referred: "Governmental units spend the money they collect as to private enterprises, and they are similarly affected by changes in the purchasing power of that money." [21]

To parody a famous remark made in another connection, the way to reduce taxes is to reduce. Regardless of what can be done to distribute the tax burden more equitably between the owners of farm property and other groups, few authorities dispute that the general

[21] Coombs, *op. cit.*, note 19, p. 5.

business situation calls for drastic governmental economies.

Also there is need of vision in the whole tax situation. Taxes are always unpopular, but a government can't be provided without someone paying the costs. The time to raise taxes and reduce the public debt is when times are good. The time when the country is least able to stand increased taxation is when business is declining. Everyone would be better off today if income taxes had not been lowered after 1920. We could have well put money into social services and debt retirement that went into new industrial plants that we did not need after 1923.

In the face of high taxes it is futile to expect the individual farmer to reduce production in spite of a large crop carry-over for the entire country. High taxes are a part of the vicious circle which leads to increased production in bad times. In order to keep off the sheriff the individual farmer is forced, as long as he can get a net return per acre, to plow another field the next year.

3. *Lowered Foreign Demand.* With the major farm staples on an export basis (*viz.*, the United States produces more than can be consumed within the country), lowered foreign demand for our farm products constitutes a barrier to agricultural recovery which relegates to secondary consideration such matters as changes in consumption, changes in population, the progress of the agricultural revolution, the decline in competition and the rise in federal, state and local taxation. Without a restoration of foreign demand, American agriculture faces a long period of painful and tragic readjustment.

In considering this problem we must bear in mind a phase of the question which is lost sight of in most discussions of the tariff. Artificial trade restraints rarely stop international trade altogether. They do lower the buying power of the nation whose products are discriminated against. Trade continues, often without a serious reduction in volume, for trade has an uncanny inclination to find a way around all trade barriers. Surplus goods either have to be sold or destroyed. Few business men care to go to the latter extreme; rather, they prefer to cut their loss by selling surplus goods for whatever they will bring.

Apologists for the American tariff commonly refute the argument that it has injured foreign demand for our surplus farm products with statistical data showing that after the passage of the Fordney-McCumber Act in 1922 the volume of our agricultural exports was little affected. Similarly, immediately after the passage of the Hawley-Smoot Act, volume fell off less than prices.

Superficially, such figures afford an effective answer to the fervid appeal of some Democratic politicians that tariffs are "destroying" our international trade. The trouble is that data of this sort proves absolutely nothing. Prices are more important than volume. As a student of the course of agricultural prices remarks:

> ". . . quantity purchased is a very indefinite and unreliable measure of demand, except in relation to some definite or fixed price. We were selling to Europe after 1920 at a price approximately one-half that prevailing only a few years previously in order to induce her to take approximately her usual volume of purchases. She took little more if any, in spite of the reduced price; and for this same volume she paid us only about half as much in total value on a gold basis."[22]

In years past the prosperity of American agriculture was supported by European demand. Even today, with

[22] Wiley, *op. cit.*, note 10, p. 160.

the European agriculture recovered to near pre-war levels, the highly industrialized nations of Western Europe constitute the world's greatest market for farm products.

To Europe goes the lion's share of all our exports of raw cotton, which comprise between fifty and sixty per cent of our total cotton crop; a large share of our exports of raw tobacco,[23] of pork and pork products, and of our surplus of grains. Wheat, rye, corn and barley are the principal grains exported from the United States. Data compiled by the United States Department of Commerce shows that in the five years ending 1930 about 14 per cent of the domestic production of wheat went to foreign countries; 20 per cent of the rye; 1 per cent of the corn; and 11 per cent of the barley. Of our total exports of wheat in such period the Department estimates possibly as much as 81 per cent eventually found its way to a European destination; 99 per cent of the rye; 43 per cent of the corn; and 98 per cent of the barley.[24]

For years Great Britain has been our best customer for American farm products; Germany, the next best. The Department of Commerce has estimated that "of the direct American exports to Europe, something over a third of the wheat and wheat flour goes to the United Kingdom, a little less of the rye and corn, and about one-half the barley." Germany ranks second "as a continental European market for United States wheat and flour, and in addition absorbs substantial quantities of American rye and barley." [25]

[23] Although about 40 per cent of our total production of tobacco is ordinarily exported abroad, a relatively small per cent of our total production of burley (about 5 per cent in 1929) is exported.

[24] U. S. Dept. of Comm. Handbook, "Grain and Grain Products in Europe and Other Major Markets," *Trade Promotion Series,* No. 131 (1932), p. 1. [25] *Ibid.,* pp. 69 and 197.

The long depression in American agriculture since 1920 and its present acute distress are intimately related to lowered demand for American farm products in the more highly industrialized nations of Western Europe.

This lowered foreign demand is due in part to economic dislocations resulting from the War and to the crushing burden of debt and taxation, also a by-product of the War. It is due even more to economic policies which have prevailed both here and abroad since the Armistice.

In this category we must include our tariff policy, debt policy and foreign policy during most of the last decade.

One serious indictment of the American protective tariff, from the agricultural point of view, is that it raises the level of costs in this country, diverting European demand for farm products to countries such as Canada, the Argentine and Australia, which are on a lower level of costs.

This change in the drift of world trade is not a new thing.

From about 1900 to the beginning of the World War, exports of United States farm products were declining, and the explanation seems to be that after 1900 the United States had gotten on a higher level of costs.

High import duties on foreign manufactured articles were a powerful stimulus to manufacturing in the United States. High tariffs, which largely excluded the competition of foreign manufactured articles, the decline in competition in industry which enabled large corporations to retain, or to distribute among their stockholders and favored officials a greater share of the economies of improved efficiency and large-scale production, and the decline in competition in labor, which enabled the latter, through the rise of the unions, to secure a larger participation in the profits of industry, were reflected in higher costs all around, higher wages, higher freight rates and shipping charges, higher distribution and middlemen's costs, higher construction costs, higher material costs. The increasing congestion of the cities was reflected in higher city rents.

Under such conditions, American agriculture, though it has at hand the world's most efficient agricultural machinery and some of the world's most fertile soil, is handicapped in competing with lands on a lower level of costs. The American producer finds it increasingly difficult to compete in the European markets with Canadian wheat and Argentine beef.

Another indictment of the American protective tariff, from the agricultural point of view, is that it invites reprisals, such as tariff duties, import regulations and license quotas, imposed, by the nations discriminated against, on American farm exports.

The most serious indictment of the American protective tariff is that the most authoritative opinion both here and abroad recognizes that its continuance on a higher level after 1922, and on a still higher level after 1930, created disturbances leading directly to the world depression and greatly aggravating its course and severity.

We cannot here undertake to unravel the tangled causes of the depression, except to explore superficially several salient phases which are intimately related to the revival of foreign demand for our goods.

The most important of these is the *impasse* which has arisen because of America's failure resolutely to face the realities of her status as the second largest creditor nation in the world. Since 1914 there has been a fundamental change in the economic position of the United States. Because of this change, logically the United States should have the lowest tariff in the world, instead of the highest. Prior to 1914 the United States was a debtor nation, owing the rest of the Old World large sums of money and sending to it in payments against principal and interest a continuous stream of products, of which farm exports were by far the largest items. At the outbreak of hostilities the net debt of the United States on international balance was approximately three billion dollars, made up largely of American securities and properties owned by Europeans.[26]

This picture changed during the War, but the abnormal demand for American farm products to feed the peoples of Europe during the War and in the period after the Armistice prevented the implications from being realized. The failure of the mass of the voters and of the responsible authorities at Washington since to recognize the consequences of the change, places upon us an invidious share of the burden for involving the whole world in economic disaster.

A nation, like an individual, must balance its payments. Disregard of this elemental economic proposition threatens the permanent destruction of foreign demand for American farm exports.

For the five years immediately preceding the War the

[26] Rogers, *America Weighs Her Gold,* p. 46. Yale University Press (1931).

exports of raw cotton alone paid our foreign bill, exceeding by $200,000,000 the balance of trade in our favor. With the change of America from a debtor nation to one of the world's largest creditor nations, thereafter it was mathematically impossible for us to go on selling the rest of the world more than we were willing to receive in payment, except by lending foreign funds with which to buy the products of our farms and factories. During the War and afterwards Europe bought from us as long as our government and private banking interests would give her credit. Had the United States not extended to the Allies her resources of capital, no less than her man-power, the Allies could hope only for a stalemate peace without victory. During the period that lasted up to early in 1920 Europe bought from us on a vast scale and sold us little. The gap in international payments was bridged with American loans.

In spite of the severe crisis in 1920–1921 and the temporary cessation of our credits to Europe, this lending was resumed and continued until 1929 in such volume that our exports even grew. We were yet to learn the lesson that a creditor nation cannot hope, without just such foreign lending, to accomplish the impossible task of collecting the money from its foreign debtors and on its foreign investments, and that on its surplus exports, while restricting the capacity of foreigners to pay us by barring their goods from our markets with prohibitive tariffs.

Yet for six and one-half years after 1922 we continued to loan to foreigners the funds for these different purposes. How this was possible and why it came to an end has been briefly summarized by Mr. Benjamin M. Anderson, Jr., economist of The Chase National Bank of the City of New York:

"A very unusual situation in the money market, due to the fact that we, almost alone of the countries of the world, were on the gold standard, and that all the free gold of the world was flowing to us, made it possible for us to expand credit on a great scale and made it possible for us to take foreign bonds on a great scale. We sent goods to the outside world and in exchange the world sent us paper, promises to pay in the future. Then the gold situation changed in 1927–28, and the money market changed in the United States. Our ability to take foreign bonds was suddenly greatly reduced, and our appetite for foreign bonds was greatly diminished. Beginning in the latter part of 1929, the ability of the outside world to buy from us sharply and violently diminished." [27]

The gold situation changed after the return of Europe to the gold standard. The money market in the United States changed because of the Wall Street boom. After the latter got beyond the control of the Federal Reserve authorities, the insatiable appetite of speculators for funds with which to buy securities to sell to someone else at a higher figure attracted short-term funds from all parts of the world. In March, 1929, call money on the New York Stock Exchange soared to 20 per cent.

Foreign lending stopped. The central banks of the Old World, in order to protect their gold reserves and maintain the parity of currencies, were forced to raise their discount rates. The effect of these influences was to curtail credit for the needs of legitimate business.

It is significant that business began to decline in Europe before it did in the United States, though by the summer of 1929 business had begun to decline in the United States.

In the collapse, like a tower of cards, of the top-heavy speculative structure in New York some months later, some authorities attach considerable importance to a rela-

[27] *Chase Economic Bulletin,* Vol. XI, No. 2 (March 23, 1931), p. 4.

tively insignificant incident. The collapse would have occurred sooner or later; but the Hatry failure in England in September, 1929, because it necessitated the sudden withdrawal of short-term credits in large volume, undoubtedly helped precipitate the October Wall Street panic.

After 1929 there followed not one crisis, but a series of crises, spreading from country to country. The volume of trade between nations throughout the entire world fell off alarmingly during 1930, 1931 and 1932. A cyclical business depression deepened into one of the great catastrophes of modern times.

Although before this book is published the United States will have undoubtedly weathered the worst of the storm, there is good ground for belief that prosperity will not permanently return to the American farm unless the United States adapts its policies to the exigencies of the world situation.

It is estimated that at the present time the United States is a long-term creditor of the rest of the world to the extent of over fifteen and a half billion dollars, not including the much talked of War Debts, amounting roughly to another eleven and a half billions more under the debt settlements as funded.

The latter will be recurred to in a later chapter. Dismissing the War Debts from consideration here, we can only sell our surplus products abroad either by resuming the extension of foreign credits or by accepting from other nations goods and services in an amount sufficient to meet accruals on this fifteen and a half billions of long-term debts, as well as the accruals on short-term funds, and to balance our surplus exports.

Since the War, except for the interruption during the crisis of 1920–1921, and until 1929, we financed our surplus exports by extending foreign credits. This appears clearly if we examine the international balance sheet of the United States for 1928, the last full year of America's illusory boom prosperity.

In 1928 we sold abroad about 850 million dollars more goods than we bought. In the same period we received about 800 millions net returns on our foreign investments. In order to get the 1,650 millions to pay us, our foreign customers and debtors got 660 millions from American tourists and 220 millions from immigrants in this country, who sent money home to the Old World. This covered little more than half of what foreign customers and debtors owed us. The balance came out of the 970 millions which we loaned them that year. In other words, we were able to sell so much more than we bought in 1928 by loaning foreigners the money to make up the difference.

This method of balancing our international payments increases the debt of other nations to us. The heavy losses which await the holders of many foreign obligations and unstable political conditions all over the world will render the resumption of foreign lending on anything like the scale from 1922 to 1929 a remote possibility in the next few years, however salutary foreign loans might be at the present time, if wisely used to finance the export of our unwanted surpluses.

Furthermore, when combined with high tariffs which restrict the ability of foreign customers and creditors to make payment, this method of balancing our international payments has a more fatal weakness in its effects as reflected in the gold situation. No nation contains within its borders all the things it needs. A creditor nation which by a high tariff restricts foreigners from paying for its surplus exports in goods and services, forces them to pay to a large extent in gold. Gold is not subject to import restrictions and moves more freely in international commerce than any other commodity. A creditor nation which adheres to a high protective tariff tends to drain the gold reserves of other nations.

The dislocation of gold may be realized from the fact that the United States and France, both of which cling to high protective tariffs in spite of their being large creditor nations, at the present time hold nearly three-quarters of the world's gold supply. Unless the tariff walls of these two countries come down, it is doubtful if the international gold standard, on which the world's business has been done in the past, can again be made to work.

A feature of the world depression has been the revelation of the connection between tariffs, debts and the money question. Early in 1933 our government listed thirty-three countries as officially off the gold standard. Upon tariff obstacles there was superimposed the difficulty of selling the surplus products of the United States to countries with depreciated currencies. Unfavorable rates of exchange, no less than our tariff, lowered the capacity of such countries to take our products. Another factor which reduced foreign demand for our agricultural products was the fluctuations in the exchange rates themselves, which increased the hazards of commerce both for our exporters and for their foreign customers. The latter continues a disruptive factor, complicated by gyrations in dollar exchange.

Until there is a revival of foreign buying power coincident with a revival of foreign demand, agriculture in the United States seems fated to remain a sick industry.

In this chapter a rapid survey has been made of various economic frontiers which confront our farm population beginning with the simpler and ranging to the more complex. The economic picture disclosed reveals the absurdity of the suggestion that any particular panacea will afford relief.

The one thing that will help more than anything else is a restoration of foreign buying power. Lowered foreign purchasing power constitutes the greatest single obstacle to lasting farm relief.

The revival of foreign purchasing power may be promoted in a number of ways; by a reduction of the American tariff, an adjustment of the War Debts or a resumption of foreign lending.

The soundest step is a reduction in the American tariff, which would enable our foreign debtors and creditors to pay for our surplus exports in goods and services. Before returning to the subject, a chapter entitled *Farm against Factory* will be devoted to gaining an historical perspective of the farm relief controversy in its political phases; and another, entitled *A Decade of Farm Relief,* to an interpretation of an era lately departed.

CHAPTER III

FARM AGAINST FACTORY

STUDENTS of the American scene recognize that with the disappearance of the physical frontier in the nineties —meaning thereby, the exhaustion of free land—the problems of the United States have become predominantly social or economic. John Dewey, the philosopher, remarks in his book, *Individualism Old and New,* "The problems to be solved are general, not local. They concern complex forces that are at work throughout the whole country, not those limited to an immediate and almost face-to-face environment."[1]

Enough has already been disclosed to show the reader that the farm problem is a problem of this sort. The individual farmer can do little or nothing about it. He is caught in the vortex of forces which he can scarcely understand, much less control. His individual efforts to meet the requirements of a new day merely add to the woes of the group. Successful improvements in efficiency, the planting of larger crops to meet the toll of higher costs and mounting taxes, cannot restore an equality of prices between what he has to sell and what he has to buy.

While coöperative marketing offers substantial benefits for certain classes and kinds of producers, it does not

[1] Dewey, *Individualism Old and New,* p. 91. Minton, Balch & Company (1929).

furnish an answer to the difficulties of others. The idea that the way to help the farmer is to encourage him to help himself through collective action was a popular one prior to the depression, when many otherwise sensible men committed what the Beards have called "the fatal error of separating economics from politics as if the production and distribution of wealth could be divorced from the civil law under which the process operates."[2] Those who shout coöperative marketing now are still living in the same comfortable illusion.

A survey of the economic aspects of the farm problem, as attempted in the last chapter, reveals how in fundamental ways the problem falls within the sphere of governmental concern. There is hardly any public problem which touches public policy and legislation at so many vital points as the farm problem.

We see that this is so when we place the present situation in an historical setting. The farmer's grievances against other groups in the population go back to the beginning of the industrial revolution, the full force of which was felt in the eastern part of the United States considerably later than in England. As the Beards, Dodd, Adams and other historians have made clear to the present generation, the tangled currents of American history become intelligible only when we correlate them with the progressive evolution of the country from an agricultural to a highly industrialized nation.

From early times the United States has contained sections and groups with conflicting economic interests.

An evaluation of the significance of the farm problem

[2] Chas. A. and Mary Beard, *The Rise of American Civilization,* Vol. I, p. 749. The Macmillan Company (1930 ed.).

at the present time calls for a frank recognition of the inescapable realities and a study of the facts of American history such as few of our public men have the courage to undertake.

Among the inescapable realities is the circumstance that the immediate self-interests of farming and those of manufacturing, transportation and finance, though interdependent, in various ways conflict. The fact is felt rather than perceived by the farmers themselves.

At the time the nation was founded nine-tenths of the entire population lived on farms, and many of the national leaders were either farmers or owned farms. Washington, Jefferson, Madison and Monroe depended in whole or in part upon the soil for their livelihood.

There was no discrimination against agriculture when the national government was in such hands.

As much cannot be said since the agricultural population became a definite minority in the nation. Since the Civil War the framework of our government has been bent from its original conception as an organ through which society protected itself against the rapacity of selfish interests, to a mechanism through which special groups, under the guise of law, have exploited those less strategically placed. In the contest for special privilege, too often the farmers' interests have been deliberately ignored or evaded by those responsible for the direction of national policies.

Although with the example of the Federal Farm Board before us a plausible, but untrue, argument can be made to the contrary, the main trend of legislation since the World War has been against the farmers.

If the reader is inclined to doubt, let him consider

some of the principal ways in which the normal level of opportunities and conditions as between agriculture and industry at the present time are distorted.

We quote a distinguished economist, Professor E. R. A. Seligman, of Columbia University:

"If there were no tariff on industrial products the farmer could secure many of his articles, both of production and consumption, at a lower price; if there were no restrictive immigration law he could secure his farm labor at a cheaper rate; if there were no adherence to outworn methods of taxation he would not now have to suffer the unfair burdens which now rest upon him; if credit conditions were as satisfactory in agriculture as in business he could secure his capital more cheaply; if freight rates were so adjusted as to put the emphasis still further upon value than upon bulk, his outlays would be reduced." [3]

While the long inequality of farming with industry needs to be remedied, candor compels the admission that, in the conflict for legislative equality, agriculture since the Civil War has won many partial victories.

So far as legislation goes, farmer votes, along with those of the small business man, furnished much of the impetus for the passage of the Interstate Commerce Act of 1887 and the Sherman Act of 1890. Political demands of the farmer revolts of a generation or so ago, such as graduated income and inheritance taxes and popular election of Senators, have long since been enacted into law. On matters more nearly related to the economic interests of the farmers may be found hundreds of acts of legislation on the statute books of the nation. One does not have to be reminded of such landmarks as the Hatch Act of 1887, providing for the establishment of experiment

[3] Reprinted from Seligman, *The Economics of Farm Relief* (1929), p. 154 with the permission of Columbia University Press.

stations in each of the several states, the creation of the Department of Agriculture in 1889, the progressive multiplication of its activities down to the present day, the rural free delivery act of McKinley's administration, the irrigation and waterway projects of the Roosevelt and later régimes, parcel posts and postal savings banks under President Taft, and the farm-credits legislation of the Wilson and Harding administrations. Nor should be omitted from this list the Agricultural Marketing Act, which became a law near the end of the Hoover honeymoon.

In spite of these acts of legislation the farmer has been fighting a losing battle with the factory.

A full account must be left to more competent historians. We shall venture here only to show how the industrial East and North became dominant in the affairs of the federal government, the inherent conservatism of the farmers' viewpoint and some of the historic areas within which the conflict of economic interest between the various groups is still obvious.

In limiting these matters to a single chapter we are compelled to stress the more colorful parts of the record, at the risk of overstating the effect of the tariff and other institutional arrangements.

By 1850 the United States had become divided into at least three well-defined sections, different in their economic structure and having different points of view, expressing the predominant self-interest of the particular section.

The economic structure of the South was that of the plantation system, dependent in a peculiar degree upon negro slavery; that of the East, upon manufacturing, which in 1850 for the first time surpassed in value the agricultural production of the nation. For thirty years and more the self-interest of these two sections had been drawing them apart. Because of its manufactures the East was becoming more and more interested in the tariff and also in the development of railroads to open up markets for the products of its factories. The South, with its production of cotton and other farm staples which were sold on the world market, was opposed to the tariff; it favored the development of railroads and other internal improvements, but was opposed to the use of federal appropriations for that purpose, as this use of government moneys served as a means for disposing of what the South regarded as an unnecessary federal surplus created by the tariff.

After the administration of President Monroe, the last of the Virginia dynasty of statesmen, neither the South nor the East was strong enough to control the national government without the support of the West. The self-interest of the latter section was primarily agricultural, but, unlike the South, it had been settled by small farmers and small merchants. The West was chiefly interested in the problems of settlement, the construction of railroads and internal improvements, a liberal policy for the disposal of the federal domain, cheap land. It was divided from the South by an inherent antipathy to slavery; from the East, by the tariff.

In 1846 a combination of the planters and small farmers forced the tariff drastically downwards, and for over ten years, while a moderate tariff level, corresponding to that of 1816, was in effect, the United States enjoyed one of the longest and most remarkable periods of development and prosperity in its history. It was a period marked by "the amazing growth of northern industries, the rapid extension of railways, the swift expansion of foreign trade to the ends of the earth" and, as was to prove so fatal to the interests of the Southern planters, "the attachment of the farming regions of the West to the centers of manufacture and finance through transportation and credit."[4]

When in 1857 the tariff was again lowered, it seemed as if the country was unmistakably headed for free trade, or at least for the permanent adoption of the general principle of a tariff for revenue only, which President Pierce a few years before had proclaimed with assurance could now be regarded "as the settled policy of the country."

The alliance of the Southern planters and Western farmers on a low tariff could not, however, hold together under the strain of the controversy over the extension of slavery. For years the West had been for cheap land, a policy that would promote the rapid settlement and building up of the country. As early as 1820 this demand had been recognized by an act providing for the sale of as small a plot as eighty acres at the price of $1.25 an acre. From 1840 onwards, while passions were becoming more heated over the question of slavery, there was recurrent agitation in Congress for additional legislation which would grant free homesteads to settlers. On this point the West was long thwarted in its desire; first by the East, where manufacturers feared that the opening up of the public domain to free settlement would drain away from

[4] Chas. A. and Mary Beard, *op. cit.*, note 2, Vol. II, p. 6.

their factories the supply of cheap labor upon which they depended; next, no less insistently, by Southern slave-owners, who, after the institution of slavery had come under fire, resisted with all the means in their power the settlement and introduction into the Union of new non-slave states.

Although in the House of Representatives many members, particularly those from districts inhabited by independent farmers, voted for free homesteads when the question first came before them, in the South, where the wealthy planters were more powerful, resistance was obdurate. The planters defeated the Homestead Bill of 1852; when in 1859 the matter was again put to a vote in Congress, only three Southern members voted in favor of the free distribution.

By this time the South had lost the support of a large section of the Western farmers. The way had been paved for a new alliance of the West with the East. The Republican party, which had its birth in the West in 1854 as a party of protest against the repeal of the Missouri Compromise and the increasing encroachments of the slave power, made its appeal, prior to 1860, largely to men who were determined to keep the public domain open to settlement by free farmers.

The veto by Buchanan, in 1860, of a measure which fixed a small price for homesteads and provided that, at the end of thirty years, any land remaining unsold should be ceded to the states helped the new party. The Western farmers and the workingmen of the East wanted free homesteads; the manufacturers wanted a tariff. In 1860 the Republican platform for the first time united the West and the East, "arousing the masses [say the Beards] with the new slogan, 'Vote yourself a farm,' while rallying the manufacturers with a kindred cry, 'Vote yourself a protective tariff.' "[5] With Abraham Lincoln, a Western candidate, the new party pledged itself to the preservation of the Union and the limitation of slavery; its success and the withdrawal of the Southern members from Congress, during the Civil War, made possible the passage of the Homestead Act of 1862 and also the creation of the kind of tariff the manufacturers wanted.

The Civil War which sundered the agricultural interests of the West and South was followed by Reconstruction. As Dunning, the historian of Reconstruction, has showed, the Republican party after the Civil War was very different from what it had been before the War. Originally it had been a party of protest, largely agrarian in origin, professing adherence to Jeffersonian tenets. After the War it became quite definitely the party of the industrialists and the financiers.

Nor was the Democratic party, after 1865, the same as it was before the Civil War. Branded with the support of treason, no wholesale assault on the Civil War tariffs was possible or likely to be attractive to the party leaders, lured by hope of spoils. In an attempt to unite the disaffected elements in the country it accepted as its candidate in 1872 Horace Greeley, an avowed protectionist. General Hancock, the military hero who was its standard-bearer in 1880, declared with realism and engaging frankness that the tariff was a local issue. Not until President Cleveland in 1887 startled the country with an unexpected message in which he announced that the protective tariff, besides being vicious and inequitable, taxed every consumer in the land "for the benefit of the manufac-

[5] Chas. A. and Mary Beard, *op. cit.*, note 2, Vol. I, p. 692.

turers," was a national election fought clearly on the merits of protectionism.

Although losing in 1888, Cleveland was returned to power four years later on the same issue and on the mistakes of the intervening Republican administration; and for two years the Democrats controlled both the executive and legislative branches of the federal government—something which had not happened since the Civil War and was not to happen again until the division of their political foes in 1912 returned them to power.

During this period, in the year after the panic of 1893, the House of Representatives made an effective breach in the protective system, but the attack failed in the Senate, where the division was closer, because of the defection of a few Democratic senators from industrial states. The amended bill proved so abortive that Cleveland, disgusted, let it become a law without his signature.

The only low tariff the country has enjoyed since the Civil War was that of the Underwood Act of 1913. Since Wilson there have been two general revisions upwards, well-known as the Fordney-McCumber and the Smoot-Hawley Acts.

Although there were many attempts to reëstablish the union of the agrarian interests of the South and West, the farmers of the South and those of the West continued after the Civil War to divide their political allegiance because they or their fathers or grandfathers fought on different sides. In the words of Professor W. E. Dodd, of the University of Chicago: "They must vote as they had shot; and children must vote as fathers had shot." [6]

[6] Dodd, "Epic of the Embattled Farmer," *New York Times Magazine*, July 24, 1927.

Since the Civil War the United States has bestowed more generous favors upon private industry than any nation of modern times. Witness the general land policy which resulted in a rapid alienation of the priceless timber, mineral and power resources of the public domain, the public grants to railroads, shipping and other private enterprises, special favors in taxation, the protection afforded to invested capital by a conservative federal judiciary which fashioned out of the cabalistic language of the Fourteenth Amendment to the Federal Constitution an effective instrument with which to strike down local experimentation in social and economic fields when to the majority of the Supreme Court the change appeared undesirable, the royal privileges vouchsafed by exclusive patents or franchises or accorded in corporate charters, and a paternalistic tariff system which has been continued after it has become an economic anachronism.

To hold the West to its established political moorings, the political party in power in 1890, when it passed the McKinley bill restoring Civil War duties, adopted the Sherman Act and a Silver Act, the latter as a gesture to satisfy the West's desire for cheap money. The Congress that raised the tariff in 1930 gave the West duties on agricultural products and the Federal Farm Board. When the panic of 1893 broke upon the country, the farmers of the South and West suffered acute distress not unlike that of today. Have they learned by the fatal mistake then made, or will they, loaded with debt now as then, repeat the mistake of more than a generation ago?

Then, as now, a continued slump in the purchasing value of the dollar was making it increasingly hard to pay debts. Then, as now, most of the farmers were in debt. As James Truslow Adams points out, in *The Epic of America,* the payment of debts has always been "of supreme importance to the West." It was a new country, and "every new country which needs development faster than capital can be accumulated locally must go heavily into debt."[7]

"If [continues Mr. Adams] during the existence of the debt, a fluctuation in the purchasing power of the currency in which payment is demanded *increases* the purchasing power of money, it is equivalent in the eyes of the debtor to an increase in his debt, an increase made by him involuntarily. If it takes two dollars to buy a bushel of wheat, a farmer can pay a one-thousand dollar debt by selling five hundred bushels, but if the value of the currency rises so that one dollar will buy a bushel, then the farmer will have to sell twice as much to pay the debt. No Western university may have boasted a chair of economics, but every farmer had firmly grasped this simple proposition. If the 'money power' . . . seemed to do anything to make money less 'cheap', it would certainly hear from the farmer."[8]

In the stirring nineties the tariff issue, on which the farmers almost won, was thrust aside in opportunistic fashion for "cheap money." Like the demand for tariff reduction, the demand for cheap money was based on a real agrarian grievance; but the money issue, as framed in 1896, was unsound economically. Both farm and factory, if they owe or are owed money, gain or lose, as the case may be, when it is cheapened. Cheapening of money (inflation of the currency), while it may help debtors, ruins creditors. Deflation of the currency operates conversely. The silver issue was not a real issue

[7] Adams, *The Epic of America,* p. 298. Little, Brown and Company (1931).

[8] *Ibid.,* p. 298.

between the farm and the factory, but rather an issue between debtors and creditors. The adoption of the issue in 1896 by the political party which could most appropriately seek relief for agrarian grievances was, in the words of Mr. Adams, "wrong, tragically wrong, as it was later to prove, for it ruined the party of protest that the nation had bitterly needed."[9]

A common fallacy is to stress agrarianism and capitalism—meaning by the latter term, manufacturing, transportation and finance—as if the two terms were antithetical. As a matter of fact the farmer is a capitalist as well as the factory owner. Farming is a form of capitalistic enterprise. A farmer cannot farm without land, livestock and machinery, which constitute his capital instead of more liquid assets.

In the aggregate, farming is the largest single form of capitalistic industry in the nation. In 1919 the investment in agriculture was greater than the aggregate of that in manufacturing industries, in mines and quarries and in railroads; the net value of all agricultural products was 40 per cent of all agricultural, mining and manufacturing production.[10]

Upon agriculture depends the future of whole states, of thousands of small towns with their local banks and local business men.

Agriculture is the mainstay of traditional American individualism against a mercantile or industrial socialism. Agricultural prejudice is an imponderable obstacle to the spread of the doctrines of communism.

Until the industrial revolution power always resided

[9] *Ibid.*, p. 300.

[10] National Industrial Conference Board, Inc., *The Agricultural Problem in the United States,* Chapter I (1926).

in the land. Until recent times most of the world's revolutions were against the landed interests.

The American farmer has never been a radical, as that term is understood in Europe. Though sometimes goaded by economic injustice to seek redress through unorthodox political panaceas, he believes in a settled order of things. Traditionally, he is a conservative, with a respect for property rights. He is a bulwark of the established American social order. In a very real sense he is one of America's last remaining individualists. In spite of the continuing concentration in industry and the drift of the farm population to the cities, American farming, in another sense, remains the foundation of the American business structure. Its prosperity quickens every other activity; its ruin threatens ruin for all.

For years agriculture asked little from government except equal laws and favoritism to none. This creed is expressed in the following words from a speech made nearly forty years ago by one dear to the author, who brought to the successful management of his farm, as well as to the solution of public questions, a mind trained to probe to the bottom of any question and an inherent passion for giving every dog his due:

> "The farmer may be always sure that when other classes are unduly favored by the government, it is done to a greater or less extent at his expense. It is exactly as when any organ or part of the body is unduly stimulated, there is always a subtraction of the blood and nutriment from the other parts of the body, and finally a detriment to the whole.
>
> "Let the government, by wise and liberal laws, give encouragement and healthy development to all interests, but no favoritism to any should be the political faith of every farmer." [11]

[11] C. M. Clay, Jr., *Selected Speeches and Writings,* p. 70. The Winthrop Press (1914).

As forty years ago, so today, agriculture has more to gain from an honest and even-handed square deal from those powerful in industry and government than from any panacea, however specious or appealing. The practical farmer senses this with an intuition in which the so-called farm leaders and professional friends of the farmer are too often deficient.

The remainder of this chapter will be devoted to matters touching the farmers' interests, which for years have been the backbone of American politics. The depression, which has revived the interest of the public in the workings of popular government, has brought out into the open once more the areas within which the agricultural and industrial points of view are in conflict. The division, needless to say, does not follow the division of political parties. It cuts deeply beneath the lines of the conventional political alliances which are held together by the lure of winning national elections.

Due to the necessity of compressing the historical background of the farm situation within a limited number of pages, the author has been forced to emphasize the relation of the tariff to the long controversy. As a matter of fact the tariff is but one of a class of questions relating to limitation of competition and price-control, in which manufacturing and distributive industries because of their centralization of control are more able to limit competition than the farmers.

The Tariff. The industrial point of view is intelligible and may be stated simply. A high tariff is a powerful stimulus for building up domestic industry. It does this by restricting and keeping out the competition of foreign goods. Tariff protection enables an industry to attain a certain amount of economic stability, insuring, if combined with monopoly aspects, a degree of stabilization of prices and profits which is unattainable where the domestic industry is subject to the shifting hazards of international competition.

As a method of price-raising it can be made fully effective only in cases where there is a domestic deficit and monopoly power which will insure that production is regulated to the capacity of the domestic market.

It can protect the farmer just as well as the manufacturer—provided these conditions are met.

From the standpoint of national interest a tariff is justifiable in order to enable industries to get a start, without which the country might be handicapped in time of war.

In addition, it is the means of establishing an infant industry, for which capital and experience are lacking.

A special case can be made out for tariffs on manufactures in a country in the condition of the United States up to about 1880. Prior to 1880 the United States was a preponderantly agricultural nation, dependent upon foreign manufacturers for various kinds of goods. The same may be true of other new countries where it may be desirable to promote a better balance of economic activity.

These are about the only valid arguments that can be made for a protective tariff system from the standpoint of the interests of a nation as a whole as opposed to the selfish interests of individuals. Economists frankly recognize that a tariff is a subsidy. Industry, through its power of organization, is able to retain a larger share of the benefits of the subsidy than was possible in a day of small farmers and petty merchants. Yet even where subsidized industries have come to dominate their respective fields, the number of those who share in the subsidy either directly or indirectly is very large.

From the standpoint of longer national interest, the only rational basis for a program of national production is furnished by the principle of comparative advantage. It is as wasteful of natural resources and of human energy for a nation to be producing things for itself that it can buy more cheaply from somebody else, as it is for an individual to do it.

An outstanding example of national waste is the subsidy to the sugar-beet growers. The absurdities to which the protective principle can be carried are shown in the proposal which has been seriously made that the United States should impose an import duty on bananas to increase the consumption of apples and thereby help the apple-growers, who can't be helped directly by a tariff because the United States produces apples for export. Other absurdities were the subsidy to silkworm culture in the United States which was in force for a generation or more; and that to tea-growing, which lasted from 1859 to 1898.

Professor John D. Black of Harvard sums up the indictment against the tariff from the standpoint of longer national interest, with a realistic view too infrequently found among university professors:

> "A system of wholesale tariff subsidy such as is fastened upon the United States is constantly benefiting a large number of groups at the expense of the rest, and to the detriment of the nation as a whole. The groups receiving subsidies are so numerous and represent so many people that they probably constitute a majority of the nation. Yet only a few groups are

probably receiving enough subsidy to repay them for their share of the loss of total national dividend which results from producing so many things at comparative disadvantage. There is not so much real conflict of interests here as a failure to understand real interests. The increases in price of particular commodities due to tariffs are much more apparent than the general losses from a tariff system." [12]

The farmer's grievance against the tariff comes principally, but not wholly, from the producers of surplus exports.

In the beginning it should be observed that even in the case of those farm-products for which a tariff can be made effective, the producers, because they lack control of production such as is possessed in some industries, cannot retain in like degree the benefits of the subsidy. Even if all the producers were organized into coöperatives and some way could be found under our Federal Constitution whereby the association might compel its members involuntarily to restrict acreage, control over production would be less effective than in monopolistic industries, due to the uncertain factors of rainfall and weather.

As a matter of fact, tariff protection for farmers is a snare and a delusion, because the farm products upon which a tariff can be made effective in the United States are relatively unimportant. Among the principal items are sugar-beets, wool, lemons, citrus fruits, dairy products, flax and eggs. With low world prices and Farm Board purchases, the tariff on wheat shut out some grades of Canadian wheat, but accentuated the movement of the latter to Europe, whence it is unmistakably driving out wheat produced in the United States.

While it is true that, because of our great domestic market of over 120 millions of people, the United States

[12] Black, *Production Economics*, p. 960. Henry Holt & Co. (1930).

exported before 1930 only ten per cent of its total production of all products, American agriculture produces about twenty per cent more than the country can consume; more than one-half of its cotton; and important percentages of its wheat and tobacco. It produces more than the country can use of corn, rye and other grains, and of pork and pork products.

As to these, the producer's complaint is the same as that of the South Carolina cotton planter in 1830 and again in 1860. He sells in a world market and buys in a protected market.

The Honorable Cordell Hull, a statesman who reflects accurately the dominant interest of the farmers in the subject, as well as the longer national interest, speaks as follows:

"Agriculture has never gone to the heart of the tariff question; but should it fail soon to do so it is destined to a state of permanent decay in this country. There is no more sound economic law than that tariffs are helpless to benefit an industry with a substantial surplus, which must be annually sold abroad in competition with important quantities of like products from other countries. The American farmer, therefore, who produces of the total agricultural output some 80 to 85 per cent of the staple agricultural products, such as corn, cotton, wheat, oats, rye, hay, lard, meat products, and tobacco, much of which must be exported, can not hope to receive any appreciable tariff benefits. The existing tariffs, on the contrary, hurt the American farmer by (1) increasing his production costs, (2) his cost of living, (3) his transportation rates on both land and sea, (4) decreasing his foreign markets and his exports, and (5) decreasing his property value by surplus congestion. The tariff is a tremendous factor in the production costs of the farmer, as it is in his living costs. There is scarcely an article which he can purchase for any purpose at a price that is not tariff-inflated. His agricultural machinery was placed on the free list while higher duties were imposed on all the materials entering into the same, and the fact that the manufacturer dominates the world compels the farmer to pay high-tariff prices just the same. While the inevitable logic of high tariffs is that home production should not exceed home consumption, ultraprotectionists are striving to expand the exports of industry while they are advising the farmer to restrict his output to the home demand. They tell him that he should be content with home markets. In the first place, the farmer's home market is secure, regardless of tariffs; secondly, of what concern is the home or any other market to the farmer unless he can sell at a price above the cost of production? The farmer is interesed in prices above all else. High-tariff advocates also tell the farmers that his collapse in 1921 was primarily due to commercial depression, whereas in truth the commercial depression was primarily due to the agricultural collapse and loss of purchasing power." [13]

A subsidy has to come out of someone's pocket. Tariff subsidies to manufacturers over a long period have resulted in the indirect transfer of wealth from the agricultural regions to the highly industrialized East and North. The transfer is no less real because it has been invisible and under the guise of law.

Were it not for the unnatural conditions which men have created for their own profit through the use of the instrumentalities of government, the United States would not be so highly industrialized as it is today; there would be fewer large fortunes in the East and North; and the South and West would be far wealthier. The tariff has ever been synonymous with special privilege.

Since 1920 high tariffs in the United States, as Professor C. A. Wiley suggests in his work, *Agriculture and the Business Cycle since 1920,* have subjected the farmer to the major burden of war deflation for the benefit of the

[13] Quoted by Bizzell, *The Green Rising,* pp. 148–149. The Macmillan Company (1926).

manufacturing classes. Because industrial Europe does not raise enough food for its needs, the natural way for it to pay for its food imports is with manufactured products. "It is very true [to quote Professor Wiley] that increased imports on our part would have tended to lower the level of prices for manufactured products to the disadvantage of producers in the United States. Nevertheless, the net effect would have been to remove that very disparity between agricultural prices and the general price-level which has been so much complained of. This would have resulted because, while prices for manufactured goods would have tended to fall on the one hand, the restoration of a healthy balanced trade with Europe would have had the effect of raising prevailing prices for farm products on the other." [14]

Transportation. The economic crisis has plunged the railroads into acute distress. A drastic falling off in business has, for the time being, destroyed the credit of even the strongest carriers. Common stocks have been selling at receivership prices; railroad bonds have been selling at 10, 25, 50 and 75 cents on the dollar. In spite of the extension of government credit various roads have had to confess an inability to pay their debts; for others, recourse to the bankruptcy law continues not unlikely.

The critical condition of the railroads is likely to obscure for those who look at the situation from the standpoint of the railroad security-holder, the grievance of the farmers. From the beginnings of the railroad age, transportation has been of utmost importance to the farmer. The reasons why this is so are obvious. The

[14] Wiley, *Agriculture and the Business Cycle since 1920,* p. 184. Univ. of Wisconsin Press (1930).

price which the producer of wheat, for instance, receives for his crop is the world price, less the cost of transportation by land and across the ocean. For instance, if wheat is selling for $1.20 per bushel in Liverpool and shipping charges are 10 cents per bushel from Chicago to New York and 10 cents more from New York to Liverpool, the Chicago price tends to be $1.00 per bushel.

In the early days the farmer was at the mercy of outsiders who seldom acknowledged their public responsibility and too often ran the railroads as a purely private promotion, offering rare opportunities for manipulative profits. For instance, in 1869, with wheat selling at 76 cents in the East, it cost the Western farmer over 52 cents for transportation, leaving him only about 24 cents for his risk and labor. As the early history of the Rockefeller fortune illustrates, the railroads also controlled the economic destiny of sections and businesses.

Regulation of the railroads by public authorities has abolished rebates and rate-discriminations between competitive shippers, but it has failed to satisfy entirely either the roads or the public which uses the roads. It has made rate-levels inelastic to changing economic conditions.

In spite of the collapse of farm prices to about half the pre-war level, it is stated that, in December, 1932, the average freight rate per ton mile was approximately 155 per cent of that in 1913. Since 1926 there has been practically no decrease in the freight rate level.[15]

We can here make only a few observations which bear upon the farmer's interest in the situation.

[15] See the Memorial Petition of the American Farm Bureau Federation and other organizations to the Interstate Commerce Commission, January 25, 1933.

No one wants to cripple the railroads in the discharge of their indispensable services to the country. On the other hand, the plight of the farmers, which is worse than that of the railroads, requires that consideration be given to an adjustment of rates on agricultural products. There are special reasons why the farmer is less able to bear high freight rates than the shippers of manufactured or processed goods.

As Herbert Quick points out in *The Real Trouble with the Farmers:*

> "The farmer ships heavy commodities, in the main. The only exceptions of any consequence of which I can think at present are butter and cheese. But wheat, cotton, all the grains, livestock, fruit, vegetables—all these things are heavy and cheap. They can not bear high freight rates. The putting of high freight rates on them means, first, ruinously low prices to the farmers, and second, high prices to consumers. It can mean nothing else.
>
> "On the other hand, the farmers must buy the heavy stuff from the mines, forests and factories—coal, fertilizers, lumber, fencing, farm machinery, lime, vehicles." [16]

The principal reason for the plight of the railroads is the decline in general business.

Another reason is the development of motor-transportation and other competitive services which can haul for a lower rate.

Another reason, in some cases, is the intolerable weight of a top-heavy capital structure.

Another reason is the heavy burden of taxation to which railroad property is subjected, and the inelasticity of taxes.

[16] From *The Real Trouble with the Farmers,* pp. 100–101, by Herbert Quick, copyright, 1924, used by special permission of the publishers, The Bobbs-Merrill Company.

Another reason is the power of the unions and the rigidity of wages.

Still another reason is the tariff. The railroads and other public utilities have little to gain from a protective tariff which increases their cost of operation without a corresponding increase in the total business done. A high tariff is a positive harm to the railroads. Not only are tariff charges reflected in a higher wage bill, but likewise because of the tariff, the railroads are forced to pay out more for materials and replacements. During 1925, we are told, the railroads consumed 22⅔ per cent of iron and steel products produced. It has been estimated that the increased tariff charges on such products, together with those on all other products consumed by the railroads, amount to nearly $200,000,000 annually.[17]

A still further reason (and one which enables tariff more readily to be passed on by the manufacturer to the railroads, and by the railroads to the shippers and the traveling public) is the decline of competition in certain lines of industry.

Because individual railroads dare not offend the large steel companies and risk losing their business, up to a recent date they were continuing to pay $43 a ton for steel rails, the same price they were paying in 1929, and the same price they have paid for nearly ten years. There is no overproduction of steel rails, because rails are rolled either on order or contract. Production is limited to four large companies which, because of lack of competition from *entrepreneurs,* are able to maintain the price artificially.

[17] See speech of C. C. Dickerson, *The Congressional Record,* Vol. 67, No. 131 (May 17, 1926), quoted by Bizzell, *op. cit.,* note 13, p. 146.

To the extent that he produces export products, the farmer's interest in ocean cargo rates is no less real than his stake in railroad freight charges.

Like the railroads, American shipping is in the doldrums. The reasons are not difficult to discover.

Like our agriculture, our merchant marine has to meet world competition on American costs. It costs much more to build a ship here than it does abroad; wages and salaries are much higher than under foreign flags and, consequently, the costs of maintenance and operation are higher.

Both our agriculture and our merchant marine are stepdaughters in the American system of high tariffs and high costs.

Taxation. The governmental needs of the individual are different in an agricultural society from those in an industrial society. In the former, most of the population either lives on farms or in small towns which depend for their livelihood upon the trade of the farmers. The self-sufficient farmer, who gets a large share of his living from his land, the independent artisan and the small town merchant can get along with a government that does little except furnish redress for wrongs, preserve order and provide for the common defense.

On the other hand, in an industrialized society nearly everybody is an employee of some sort. The life of the individual is more precarious. He is a cog in a great machine. His job and his very existence becomes a matter of governmental concern. It is necessary for the government to intervene in countless ways to safeguard or provide for his health, safety and welfare.

The industrialization of the nation tends to broaden

the base of both the national and local state and city governments. Hence, even if we could eliminate governmental waste and extravagance, there does not seem to be much hope over the long term that the legitimate costs of government will decrease as the years pass, as long as the drift to the cities continues unchecked. Where once there were thousands of individuals engaged in trades and little businesses of their own, we now have great centralized industrial plants. Where once nine-tenths of the people lived on farms, now less than one-third do.

However much we may deplore the trend, the federal government is becoming increasingly a government of bureaus and commissions made necessary by the needs of a complex national life. While, if our government is to survive in substance as well as in form, a discriminating resistance is required to the centralizing tendencies of the age, government must be molded to meet conditions rather than theories. Although an outmoded conception of States' Rights is frequently used by prominent industrialists to resist the interference of the national government with the affairs of powerful nation-wide corporations, the appropriations for such instrumentalities as the Interstate Commerce Commission, the Federal Trade Commission and a host of lesser bureaus and commissions, cannot be restricted without inviting a return of abuses of an earlier age of unrestricted *laissez faire*. Chambers of commerce may adopt solemn resolves deprecating the intervention of government in the domain of business, yet there is no group in the community that expects more, or comes to the government for assistance sooner, in time of crisis, than the leaders of big business.

The trend is precisely similar in the case of state and

local governments. The intense concentration of population in cities has resulted in the growth of zoning and city planning boards, traffic, police, factory and health and welfare boards and commissions, entrusted in many cases with bureaucratic powers and touching intimately property and personal rights. Crime, fire and disease are greater risks in urban than in country districts. The regulation of utilities (other than transportation) is of greater concern to the general public in the highly industrialized states than in the farming regions.

Since the horse-and-buggy age, numerous government services have been added, but in most states we still cling to antiquated tax laws. In a simpler society, when most property was in tangibles, which could not easily escape the eyes of the assessor and tax-collector, the general property tax furnished an equitable basis of taxation.

In the new world in which we are living, much the larger share of the national income is received either in salaries, commissions and fees, on which the recipients are subject to income but not property taxes; or as dividends or interest on stocks and bonds which, though subject to the general property tax, too often escape the eye of the assessor.

How great in recent years has been the disparity in incomes, and how exaggerated has been the concentration of wealth in the hands of a few, is disclosed by the figures of the federal government. According to the Statistical Abstract of the United States for 1932, 513 men with net incomes of $1,000,000 each or over, had, in the aggregate, a net income of $1,212,000,000. On the other hand, in 1930 the farm price of American wheat was $514,847,000, and of American cotton, $659,455,000. If we add these two figures together we find that the two chief agricultural crops in the United States brought to the growers an amount less than the net income of the 513 super-rich men in the preceding year. In other words, 513 individual citizens could have bought with their net profits of the preceding year the entire 1930 wheat and cotton crops of a country with 123,000,000 population.

With values and incomes cut to the bone on all sides after three years of economic depression and panic, there is scarcely any political problem which transcends in importance that of taxation. After a steady increase for a generation or more, and with little prospects of relief in the near future, due to the numerous demands for emergency relief, the question of the proper distribution of the unhappy burden is no less important than the question of to what extent governmental expenses can be reduced and two chief sources of unnecessary expense, waste and lavish expenditure, eliminated.

It is quite possible that unprotected agriculture cannot survive if it is burdened with the support of governmental services which are or threaten to become indispensable in a highly industrialized community. Tax laws in many states need a thorough overhauling. Land is being taxed to death. The general property tax, or the way it works under present conditions, seems to be the chief cause of the trouble.

According to the figures of Dr. Whitney Coombs, senior agricultural economist of the Division of Agricultural Finance, United States Bureau of Agricultural Economics, the general property tax accounted for 83 per cent of the total state and local tax collection of the country in the year 1922. In thirteen states the percentage ran above 90 per cent.[18] Dr. Coombs estimates that three-fourths of the property reached by the general property tax is in the form of real estate, and so, assuming that the general property tax supplies 75 per cent of the total state and local tax collections, then real estate is contributing between 55 per cent and 60 per cent of such collections.[19]

These figures are impressive if we contrast with them the statement of Governor Lowden, citing an estimate of Professor John R. Commons' made several years ago, that, in the United States as a whole, the ownership of property, both tangible and intangible, accounted for not more than 20 per cent of the total net income of the population.[20]

Dr. Coombs attempted to summarize the relation of taxes to the earnings of agricultural property on the basis of intensive studies made in fourteen widely separated states. It was his conclusion that in 1927 taxes were taking about 30 per cent of the net rent of farm real estate. The situation is apparently worse in the highly industrialized North Central states, where the costs of government run high. Thus in the period 1921–1927 taxes were taking nearly 60 per cent of the net rent of farm real estate in Michigan; over 50 per cent in New Jersey.[21]

As in the case of so many questions of vital public concern, the immediate interests of the farm and of the

[18] Coombs, "Taxation of Farm Property," *U. S. Dept. of Agric.*, Tech. Bull. No. 172 (1930), p. 70.

[19] *Ibid.*, p. 71.

[20] Lowden, *N. Y. State Bar Ass. Bull.*, Oct. 1929, p. 359.

[21] Coombs. *op. cit.*, note 18, p. 66.

factory in the matter of taxation are opposed. It is in the selfish economic interest of each that the other should bear the greater share of the costs of government. This antagonism is one that has existed from the early days of the Republic, but it has deepened as the costs of government have mounted with the progressive widening of government activities during the past forty years.

In many states the lines of cleavage may be detected in divisions over practically every revenue issue of importance.

In the case of the federal government they are apparent whenever the question arises whether Congress should levy on individual incomes or resort to indirect taxes which in greater or less degree can be shifted either to the consumer or the raw producer. The income tax amendment to the federal Constitution was in large measure the work of the agrarians and the urban proletariat, as was the federal income tax law of 1894, nearly a generation before.

Since the World War, Congress has been a battleground for determining on what shoulders should fall the greater share of the legacy of public debt contracted for in the war-time period with the war-time dollar. During the reign of Secretary Mellon the general drift was towards lowering taxes on incomes while increasing tariff duties and leaving undisturbed other forms of indirect taxation.

This policy received a sharp check in the last Congress. The manufacturer's sales tax, in spite of the strongest of support in the industrial East, was defeated, in part, because of opposition based on the intelligent ground that in a period of destitution among the poorer classes, a tax which bears hardest upon small incomes which must be used up in the purchase of necessities, is, as Professor E. R. A. Seligman remarks, one of "the most indefensible revenues"; [22] in part, because of the fear engendered that the proposal was in reality intended as an entering wedge with which income taxes, at least on the higher brackets, could later be sabotaged. In short, alarm was felt by the leaders of the revolt in the House that, if adopted as an emergency measure, the new tax would be difficult to get rid of when once the emergency was over. There was a real danger that the emergency rate would be continued permanently.

As opposed to the industrialist viewpoint, which has less to fear from indirect taxes, the agrarian stands to gain from high taxes on incomes and inheritances, as contrasted with low tariff and excise taxes. Rightly, or wrongly, he reasons, from the standpoint of self-interest, that the bulk of the costs of governing an industrialized society should fall on those to whom go the profits, rather than on those who escape the income tax because they do not have enough income to tax.

Anyone who doubts the conflict between the industrialist and the agrarian points of view should consider the alignment in the Senate on the amendment proposed by Senator Couzens to the 1932 Revenue Bill, which would have restored the highest war-time rates on big incomes. While there were votes against this measure from the agrarian South and West, most of the support for it came from that region. Its defeat was due to the fact that not more than half a dozen votes were cast for it from the more highly industrialized states of the North and East.

[22] Seligman, "Toward a New Tax Program," *The Nation*, April 27, 1932, p. 485.

The Control of Monopoly. At the present time the federal anti-trust laws are in eclipse. There is respectable authority for the view that monopoly in various lines of business is not only inevitable but desirable, because of the wastefulness of unbridled competition. A special case can be made out for monopolistic control of natural resources such as coal, oil and gas, which are squandered under a system of competitive exploitation.

Regardless of whether or not the federal anti-trust laws are outmoded, it must be admitted that back of the farmer's old cry against the "trusts" there is a very real economic grievance—the injustice of a price-system which is half-competitive and half-monopolistic.

The trouble with the situation is that repeal of the Sherman Act, or its substantial modification, in order to permit curtailment of production to relieve emergency conditions among various producers, is fraught with serious danger to the general public. Human nature does not change much from generation to generation. As in the nineties, so today, the object of every combination is to maintain prices at the point which will yield the greatest profits.

In the preceding chapter we have already referred to the peculiar ways in which a partly rigid price-system works hardship upon the farmers during a general fall in prices. The severity of the present depression and the slowness of recovery is attributable in part to the unevenness of declines in the prices of different commodities. The area of rigid or inelastic prices in the last few years has probably been larger than ever before in the history of the country. It is not surprising, therefore, that prices have declined far more unevenly than in the depression of

1907–1908 or in that of 1920–1921. Furthermore, the severest declines have come in the wrong groups, particularly in farm commodities, which were already depressed. Pegged or artificially maintained prices not only prolong the completion of the liquidating process, but constitute a major obstacle to the restoration of buying power by the depressed groups.

The existence of this condition is responsible for the demand that is voiced by the more radical farm groups that the farmer should be guaranteed the cost of production.

Most of the pressure for the repeal of the federal anti-trust laws, on the other hand, comes from big industry. We are even told that the law is an obstacle to economic recovery, if not a cause of the business depression. Typical of this attitude is the following utterance of Thomas L. Chadbourne, a world-famous lawyer accustomed to large corporate affairs:

"Repeal, or at least amendment, of the Sherman act, is a fundamental and economic reconstruction. It is a menace to our economic structure. As it stands it effectually ties the hands of the industrialists of the nation who are working to curb the calamity of over-production and unwieldly surpluses.

"Unless the American people awake to the necessity of amending our laws in so-called restraint of trade, the present depression may be expected to remain with us or to recur as a chronic disaster." [23]

The movement likewise has the support of many who look at the matter from the standpoint of the regularization of employment and of wages rather than of profits. Such is the professed objective of the so-called Swope

[23] Reprinted by permission from *The Swope Plan,* by Gerard Swope (now published as *Readings in Economic Planning*) The Business Bourse (1931), pp. 73–74.

Plan, named after Mr. Gerard Swope, the President of the General Electric Company. This proposal contemplates that all companies in the electrical manufacturing business, employing more than fifty persons and doing an interstate trade, should be permitted to form trade associations for the purpose of stabilizing production to the end that employment may be stabilized and effective insurance provided for employees. Recognizing that the stabilization of production necessarily implies stabilization of prices, the Swope Plan provides for protection of the public interest against price-profiteering by placing supervision of the trade associations with a federal authority.

What both the radical farm leaders who are pressing for guaranty by the federal government of the cost of production and the industrialists who are demanding license from the government to restrict output and fix prices, have failed to follow through clearly are the social and political implications of the matter.

Both proposals involve either governmental price-regulation or the extension of the public utility concept throughout major lines of industry.

The shortsightedness of the farm groups is more excusable than that of the business leaders, because of the farmer's harder necessity and lack of trained knowledge. The shortsightedness of the business leaders who are enthusiastic converts of the Swope Plan consists in that the restriction of industrial production and the lifting of industrial prices all along the line calls logically for the erection at Washington of effective mechanisms of price-control as a protection against price-profiteering.

The inconsistency into which the latter were betrayed, furnished *The Outlook* occasion for the following reflections soon after the announcement of the Swope Plan:

"It is amusing to note that the Swope plan has drawn either sympathetic or ardent comment from many conservative individuals and publications whose every previous utterance had faced in a directly opposite direction. This, we suppose, is but another illustration of the fact that conservatives can with perfect impunity advocate ideas which would get radicals shot at sunrise. What shall we say of those individuals who for years have been shouting that the government should stay out of business and now shout as loudly for the Swope plan? The Swope plan, which, going full blast, would put the government into every business there is, which, in fact, promises to put the government so far into business and business so far into government that the two would soon be one and indistinguishable! What shall we say of those individuals who bemoan bureaucracy, the centralization of power at Washington, the growth of paternalism, the decline of the rights and duties of the states, the narrowing of local self-government, and the invasion of personal liberty and then a moment later advocate a plan which stands for everything they oppose? We take it that in the last analysis the government would make it its business to fix prices under the Swope plan and that business would therefore set out to fix the government. In the end we might have commodity prices determined at the polling booth."[24]

In the whole discussion of the need that has arisen for "liberalization" of the anti-trust laws, there has been too little presentation of the stake of the farmers and of the general consuming class in the matter.

Liberty to restrict output and to fix prices, which is the real objective of the industrialists who rail at the anti-trust laws, means in most industries higher prices for the things which farmers and the public have to

[24] Quoted in *The Swope Plan, supra,* note 23, pp. 88–89.

buy. If such a situation could be achieved throughout all parts of the economic structure, the result would be a lowering of the standard of living of the people generally. This is well stated in an editorial in *The New Republic* of November 11, 1931:

"If . . . we imagine that private business should achieve control of production all along the line, industry by industry, we imagine a dangerous and intolerable situation. Each industry would be organized to restrict production in the interest of price maintenance. This would mean, to be sure, stable if not rising prices. But it would also mean a competitive restriction of the supply of goods upon which the life of the people depends. Each industry, to keep its bargaining power in the general situation, would be tempted to turn out fewer and fewer goods. Such a system would run head-on against the social need for abolishing poverty, for a rising standard of living, and against the inherent trend of machine civilization itself toward larger productivity. It is quite possible that certain industries are equipped to produce more of their special products than could be consumed by the world's population, no matter how much money we had with which to buy them. But it is absurd to say that this is true of all industries at once. However much 'overproduction' may annoy us during a depression, it is still, in the large, overproduction relative to existing purchasing power and not overproduction relative to needs and wants."[25]

The truth is that here again, as in such matters as the tariff, transportation and taxation, the immediate interests of the farm and the factory are in conflict.

Agricultural production depends less on the acreage than on the accidents of the seasons. "For ten crops over a period of 50 years," says Mr. L. H. Bean, of the United States Department of Agriculture," the yearly changes in yield, which are largely determined by climatic factors . . . have been at least six times as great as the

[25] *The New Republic,* November 11, 1931, p. 338–339.

yearly changes in acreage." [26] It depends upon the hazards of weather and rainfall, not to mention such incalculables as army worms, grasshoppers, the boll-weevil and the black rust.

Factory production, on the other hand, is subject in a much greater degree to human control. Output can be drastically limited and prices raised provided the threat of competitive price-cutting is removed. Mergers, combines, trade associations and organized restriction of output, are accordingly, the industrialist's prescription for our social ills. Not only does he want a free hand to restrict output and hold up prices, but his training and outlook lead him to advise the wheat and cotton farmers to seek the same ends. Too often he indulges in disparaging comments on the intelligence of the farmers when they fail to heed his advice to apply industrial principles to agriculture.

The control of monopoly is a question which it will take many years to settle. We hold no brief for the Sherman Act. It has been largely a failure, and the reason is that it runs counter to what appears to be an irreversible economic trend. In the forty years that the Act has been on the statute books, big business has spread out and occupied all the major lines of industry. It cannot be said, as some critics assert, that the Act has failed to stay the underlying trend, because of lack of enforcement, since the attempts to enforce the Act during the Roosevelt-Wilson period were largely a failure.

Repeal of the so-called laws to prevent the restraint

[26] Quoted in *The American Economic Review,* Vol. XXI, No. 3 (Sept., 1931), p. 446.

of trade (of which the Sherman Act is a part) will not, on the other hand, solve the problem to remedy which these laws were originated. That problem is the control of monopolistic discriminations and profiteering prices.

Their suspension does bring measurably nearer the day when price-regulation or government ownership in many lines of business heretofore classed as private will be required by popular demand to protect the interests of the consuming public.

Unless we are prepared to have the government take over the operation of our giant corporations, there is no real reason why nation-wide corporations, whose dominant position is due to the possession or control of some special natural resource or essential agency of production, transportation or distribution, should not be subject to regulation as thoroughgoing as that provided for national banks or insurance companies.

Over the near-term, the interest of the farmers, which here coincides with that of the consuming class in general, would seem to be in the preservation of free markets, and of a free price system, except in those lines which the courts must inescapably be constrained to hold are to be classed in the ever-widening field within which price-regulation is necessary in the general public interest.

With respect to those industries, in which the dominant group depends for its strategic industrial advantage upon a high tariff rather than upon the direct or indirect control of an essential element of production, transportation or distribution, there remains the neglected remedy of a gradual withdrawal of the tariff duty. The best evidence that our tariff rates are too high is the fact that finished manufactured goods are all but excluded from the United States, amounting to but 2 per cent of our imports in 1929.[27]

Lowering the tariff on imports of manufactured goods will, at any rate, curb the misdirection of capital into (1) industries which could not be kept alive and profitable without tariff subsidies and (2) industries which are helped to greater profits than before by tariff subsidies. It will also enlarge the capacity of the industrial nations of Europe, for years the principal market for American exports of farm products, to sell directly in the United States their exports of manufactures. Because these nations have, in the main, only manufactured products to export, their international payments, in the last analysis, have to be balanced by the export of such products.

It is significant that in some of our most efficient industries, such as automobiles in the field of production, and department stores and mail-order houses in the field of distribution, the position of the dominant units does not depend either upon the possession or control of some essential element of production or distribution or upon tariff protection. These, along with the farmers, stand to benefit in the long run from the gradual withdrawal of tariff duties.

[27] *Cf.* Hansen, *Economic Stabilization in An Unbalanced World,* p. 79, Harcourt, Brace and Company (1932).

CHAPTER IV

A DECADE OF FARM RELIEF

THROUGHOUT the farm relief controversy in the United States during the past decade, public discussion has centered about the problem of the agricultural surplus.

The direction of discussion into this channel has been unfortunate, as the farm problem is not one problem but many problems. The causes of agricultural depression are complex and not easily isolated. In many matters there is a direct conflict of interest between the farmers in the aggregate and industry in general. While generalization is particularly dangerous, this much can at least be said—that the depression in farming, which continued throughout America's era of bootstrap prosperity, is due, in no small degree, to the fact that for many years industry has won the greater share of legislative favors and, in the matter of the tariff in particular, has been subsidized at the expense of the unprotected farmers. It is equally clear that, if farming is not to sink into permanent decay, governmental measures are necessary which will restore to agriculture some of its lost advantages. Industry must either give up some of the advantages which it has gained, or else means must be employed which will tend to equalize agriculture with more favored forms of economic activity.

All the various proposals which have been made or adopted within the past decade, artificially to raise the price to the producer of farm products, have assumed a high protective tariff as the settled policy of the country. Though obscured in much of the popular discussion of the subject, this assumption underlies the various abortive measures for surplus-disposal which have engaged public notice.

In the case of export commodities, where there is a domestic surplus, the price received by the producer for that portion of the total production sold on the home market is determined by the world price. It is a truism that the tariff cannot be made effective on most major farm staples, such as cotton, wheat, tobacco, pork products, etc., because these commodities are, except under extraordinary conditions, sold at a price fixed by the world market.

Agriculture is the exposed flank of the American protective system. The agricultural surplus, in the sense that it is a problem, is not the root of the disease, but one of the ways in which a subtle disease manifests itself.

In many circles it is the fashion to blame the farmer's woes upon over-production. A great deal of theorizing attributes the disastrous slump since 1929 to the same plausible hypothesis.

No single theory satisfactorily explains the world-wide economic collapse. As with previous economic derangements, the great deflation is due to a combination of circumstances; its severity results from a concatenation of causes. The search for a single all-embracing cause appears singularly futile and profitless.

Perhaps the most striking economic phenomenon of the period has been the drastic world-wide decline in the general commodity price level.

For this decline the current popular shibboleth of over-production does not provide a satisfactory explanation. In it over-production of basic commodities has, of course, played a part, but able economists regard over-production as a symptom rather than a cause. An excellent case can be made out of under-consumption, both here and abroad.

Thus, as Dr. L. C. Gray, of the United States Bureau of Agricultural Economics, points out, the agricultural plant in this country has not been materially expanded since 1920, although a somewhat higher level of efficiency has been obtained. Between 1919 and 1924 there was an actual decrease of about thirteen million acres. For the most part the net expansion since 1924 has been little more than an increase in acreage of cotton, although our population has increased about 17 per cent since 1920.[1]

The production of corn in the United States in 1920 was abnormally short because of drouth, but corn fell in price. There has been no marked over-production of corn, beef-cattle, or of hogs, but prices have fallen violently. The number of beef-cattle and of hogs on farms, compared with the average, is not excessive.

The index of the physical volume of production in the United States prepared by Mr. Carl Snyder, economist of the Federal Reserve Bank of New York, which has been accepted generally by leading economists, shows that since 1865 the normal increase in the United States has been about 4 per cent per year. From other data it is estimated that the normal annual increase in the rest of the world has been about 3 per cent. In a paper read

[1] Gray, "Overproduction and Agricultural Depression," *Pro. Acad. of Pol. Sci.*, Vol. XIV, No. 3, *Depression and Revival* (June, 1931), p. 66.

at the semi-annual meeting of the Academy of Political Science in April, 1931, Mr. Snyder reached the conclusion that "in practically every line—with two or three notable exceptions—the price of war was a blasting of growth from which we have only recently recovered and that, as for the years immediately preceding the crash of 1929, the idea of an unusual rise in total production is largely a fiction." [2]

Wheat and cotton are the two agricultural commodities commonly supposed to be most over-produced in the United States.

The following estimates of actual harvests within the United States from 1913 on, taken from the Department of Agriculture, speak for themselves:

COMBINED YIELD OF SPRING AND WINTER WHEAT			COTTON	
Year	*Acreage*	*Bushels*	*Year*	*Bales*
1932 *	55,177,000	727,000,000	1932	12,727,000
1931	54,949,000	892,271,000	1931	17,096,000
1930	59,210,000	863,430,000	1930	13,931,597
1929	60,756,000	809,000,000	1929	14,824,861
1928	55,790,000	914,800,000	1928	14,477,874
1927	58,583,000	878,500,000	1927	12,956,043
1926	56,337,000	831,000,000	1926	17,977,374
1925	52,225,000	676,000,000	1925	16,103,679
1924	52,364,000	862,627,000	1924	13,627,936
1923	58,308,000	797,381,000	1923	10,139,671
1922	62,317,000	867,598,000	1922	9,762,069
1921	63,696,000	814,905,000	1921	7,953,641
1920	61,143,000	833,027,000	1920	13,439,603
1919	75,694,000	968,279,000	1919	11,420,763
1918	59,181,000	917,100,000	1918	12,040,532
1917	45,489,000	636,655,000	1917	11,302,375
1916	52,316,000	636,318,000	1916	11,449,930
1915	60,469,000	1,025,801,000	1915	11,191,820
1914	53,541,000	891,017,000	1914	16,134,930
1913	50,184,000	763,380,000	1913	14,156,486

* *Preliminary.*

[2] Snyder, "Overproduction and Business Cycles," *Pro. Acad. of Pol. Sci.,* Vol. XIV, No. 3, *Depression and Revival* (June, 1931), pp. 26, 30.

According to Mr. Snyder, the much-talked-of excess carry-over of wheat in the world is an increase of the normal carry-over equivalent to little more than three weeks' normal consumption.[3]

The relatively weak economic position of American agriculture would seem to be a matter less of over-production than of under-consumption, both here and abroad. There is over-production of wheat, cotton and tobacco in this country, but it is a sign not that the world is producing too much but distributing too little. In justification of this statement we need only mention that near half of the world lives on a meager subsistence of rice or the like that we would scarcely call a fair meal. As Mr. Snyder remarks, hundreds of millions in India and China maintain families on the equivalent of something like twelve or fifteen cents per day; and almost every year some millions die of hunger, and many are dying now. With our own large body of unemployed there are many who do not get enough to eat. To all these people the idea of too much food in the world is a hollow mockery.[4]

Without necessarily adopting Mr. Snyder's theory of the cause of the collapse in prices since 1929, we can fairly say, upon analysis, that over-production is not responsible for the part popularly assigned to it. Both over-production and under-consumption are phases of the same thing—dependent upon which side of the supply-demand equation you look at.

We can also fairly say that the prospect for a restoration of American agriculture is intimately related to the reduction of unemployment and the return of general

[3] *Ibid.*, p. 8.
[4] *Ibid.*, p. 8.

business prosperity in the United States. So far as export-staples are concerned, still more is it dependent upon foreign conditions and the return of a more normal foreign demand.

The agricultural "surplus" became widely recognized as a problem in the United States with the collapse in 1920–1921 of the Enropean demand for American farm products. With the slow recovery to a pre-war status of European agricultural production, together with the inroads made on the European market by low-cost countries like Canada, Australia and the Argentine, the "surplus" has been a problem for the American farmer ever since.

With a rapid decline of commodity prices in 1920, the farmer was in acute distress before the end of the Wilson administration. Except for the revival of the War Finance Corporation, with a direction to assist in the financing of the exportation of agricultural products, which was passed over President Wilson's veto, and the Intermediate Credits Act, which became a law under President Harding, congressional activity at the start centered upon tariff increases, the emergency act of 1921 being followed by the Fordney-McCumber Act in the following year. In both of these acts substantial (though in many cases ineffective) duties were imposed upon agricultural imports.

With the passage, in addition, of the Packers and Stockyards Act, the Grain Futures Act and the Agricultural Credits Act, all in August, 1921, Congress in the words of Professor J. D. Black of Harvard University, "had played its full bag of tricks."[5] But not for long.

[5] Black, *Agricultural Reform in the United States,* p. 74. McGraw-Hill Book Co. (1929).

The tide of agricultural discontent was reflected in the formation, largely along non-partisan lines, of the agricultural bloc; and with the continuance, throughout most of the decade, of agrarian depression, the struggle between the representatives of the farmers in Congress and the Executive forms a significant narrative that colors the balance of the Harding and Coolidge administrations. This dispute, with the passions which it aroused and with the fortunes of battle varying from one side to the other, is still fresh in memory. Instead of relating the successive stages of its development, we shall confine our attention to the divergence of viewpoint that before long became manifest. There is import in the circumstance that the leading actors in the play proceeded upon the assumption that a high protective tariff was the settled policy of the country. The McNary-Haugen or equalization-fee plan which appears to have had its birth in 1922 in a pamphlet attributed to George N. Peek and Hugh S. Johnson, at that time president and counsel respectively for the then distressed Moline Plow Company, was expressed as a design to provide "equality for agriculture in the benefits of the protective tariff." Peek had the idea that "the fair exchange value of the crop is reduced in the exact proportion with the protection afforded industry. . . . Either agriculture must die, or a way must be found so to revise protection as to insure agriculture a fair exchange value for its crops. . . . Free trade is unthinkable." President Coolidge's agricultural conference in the winter of 1924–1925 among its major recommendations stressed the need of higher tariff duties on farm products; and the President himself, in an address before the American Farm Bureau Federation in Chicago in March, 1925, defended the tariff as a boon to agriculture. By the latter date the opposing lines in Congress had become drawn, and the agricultural bloc, which had swung in line in support of price-raising by government action, had begun to play a determining rôle in shaping the course of legislation affecting the farmers' interests.

Before discussing the central ideas back of the various price-raising schemes of this period, we shall first turn our attention to another major tenet of the administration program.

Beleaguered by steadily increasing support in Congress in favor of some scheme that would "make the tariff effective for agriculture," President Coolidge, both in his opening messages to Congress and in his successive vetoes of the McNary-Haugen bills of 1927 and 1928, emphatically took the stand that in coöperative marketing lay the principal hope of agriculture.

The common sense back of this idea calls for greater consideration than we can here afford to give of the possibilities and limitations of the coöperative movement. So much has been written on the advantages to be gained by associational effort in promoting a better system of distributing and marketing agricultural products, that we must refer the reader to the literature on the subject, which is enormous. The need and desirability of government encouragement of the movement are set forth in the following passage from an article by Secretary Jardine in *The Farm Journal:*

"My position on government and coöperation, in short, is that the government should help farmers to help themselves through coöperative effort to market their products in an orderly manner, to adjust production to demand as far as possible, and to reduce price fluctuations by some workable and safe means of handling surpluses. . . . Large-scale organization for orderly marketing and for adjusting production to demand is essential to that economic stability of agriculture which we all hope to attain. To deny the farmer such opportunities for organized self-help as I have just indicated would be to deny him that opportunity of collective bargaining which is enjoyed in one form or another by other groups. . . . Producers must be willing to build from the bottom up. They must forget any petty quarrels between local leaders and organizations, and federate their locals into regional and national organizations handling large volumes of business. The best minds, experienced in the trade, must head such organizations. With such a set-up, the Government could do much more than it has done. . . . Old as farming is, large-scale merchandising by farmers, which appears essential to future agricultural prosperity, is in fact an 'infant industry.' It deserves such sound assistance as will enable it to help itself toward growth and increased efficiency. We have steadily encouraged efficiency in agricultural production. We have, through scientific research, enabled farmers to grow several grains of wheat or corn where one grew before. We should not diminish our efforts in this direction, but we should go as far as necessary to make it possible to market the extra grains to the best advantage of the producer. . . . I have not the slightest fear that such activity on the part of coöperatives would be detrimental to the public interest. On the contrary, I believe that it would be beneficial to the public to reduce price fluctuations of farm commodities by minimizing the likelihood of recurring surpluses and shortages in the market."[6]

The conspicuous success of several of the better known coöperative organizations, run on strictly business lines, requires that the limitations of the coöperatives be carefully kept in mind. Much that has appeared about coöperative marketing has been written by those who have never followed a plow. There is no question that the idea has been overworked. Disillusionment is some cases has

[6] Quoted by Black, *op. cit.*, note 5, p. 338.

followed because the farmers have been led to expect more from coöperative organizations than the situation justified. Within its legitimate sphere a coöperative organization furnishes a medium of economies in central marketing and distribution. Professor Black, a competent authority, in answer to a request to estimate the probable gain from the integration of large-scale central marketing organizations within the state of Minnesota, put the average figure at not over 5 per cent a year, and in his book *Agricultural Reform in the United States,* published in 1929, states that events proved this prediction to be too optimistic.[7] Too often the farmers have been led to regard coöperative organizations as a means of price-raising rather than of combining bargaining power and eliminating losses to the producer in selling and distribution. Coöperatives have failed because of their inability to control production, both of their own members and of farmers outside the organization. Without the power to exercise coercion over production, the stimulative effect of higher net returns often creates a danger of declining prices so great as to threaten to wreck the coöperative association. This hazard is, of course, greater where a non-perishable product is handled, and the coöperative association, acting as agent for its members, engages in the business of pooling and holding their crops in order to put them on the market when prices are most favorable. Probably no coöperative organization in the United States was directed with more executive and business ability than the Burley Tobacco Growers' Association, with over 120,-000 members in several different states, yet it was allowed

[7] Black, *op. cit.,* note 5, p. 345.

to lapse because of its inability to control the increased production, both of members and non-members, stimulated by the increased net returns received by the producers.

So far as farm staples like corn, wheat and cotton are concerned, the difficulties of coördinating the producers into associational activity on a national scale may be reckoned as well-nigh insuperable. The very size of the nation makes the idea impracticable.

Lewis F. Carr in *America Challenged* aptly says:

> ". . . there are corn growers in every rural county of every state, about five million all told, and you couldn't very well get them together. There are almost two million cotton farmers scattered from the Potomac to the Rio Grande. There are a million two hundred thousand growers of wheat, scattered everywhere. Further, corn and wheat are not the only eggs in the basket with most farmers, but parts of a rotation. If a million and a quarter farmers depended solely on wheat for a livelihood, as citrus growers depend on citrus, then there would be more likelihood of combined action. But the history of coöperative action does not justify the conclusion that it would be possible or practical even then to bring such widely scattered growers together." [8]

Coöperative marketing has been largely abandoned with tobacco and potatoes. Until the advent of the Farm Board and the policy which it followed of encouraging, with loans of government money, the organization of coöperatives, coöperative marketing made little headway with cotton and wheat. According to the figures of Professor Black, only 6.5 per cent of the total 1927–1928 cotton crop was handled by coöperatives; the eight central marketing associations operating wheat pools in 1928

[8] Carr, *America Challenged,* p. 264. The Macmillan Company (1929).

handled but 12,000,000 bushels of the record 914,000,000 bushel crop of that year.[9]

Nor in the case of the latter crop, at least, does it seem that much benefit to the growers can be expected from the application of the coöperative idea.

Says Jesse E. Pope in *Economic Essays,* published for the American Economic Association in 1927, in honor of John Bates Clark:

". . . the difficulties encountered in increasing the price of coffee, sugar and raisins above the market are as nothing compared to the difficulties of securing a super-market price for a staple crop like wheat.

"Wheat is a prime necessity. It is grown and consumed over practically the entire civilized world. Its consumption is not materially affected by either sentiment or agitation. It is grown in almost all climes by a vast number of farmers; and any slight stimulant, such as an increase in price, readily brings about an increased production. It is non-perishable and lends itself easily to transportation. It is bought and sold freely on the exchanges on the world. Every shred of information concerning existing supplies, prospects for future supplies, condition of growing crops, strength of demand, etc., is eagerly sought; and an army of experts are constantly at work supplying this information. In a word, wheat is grown and consumed in all parts of the world and its price is fixed in a world market. Therefore when an attempt is made to raise the price above the market, difficulties of all sorts are met at every turn. The domestic price, if it be above the market, can be maintained in the face of foreign grain only by a high tariff. The resulting exportable surplus must be sold at a loss on the markets of the world and since, from the very nature of things, the undertaking is too great for private enterprise, such a scheme can not be put into operation except by the Government. . . . Production must be regulated; otherwise the supply will swamp the price fixing machine. The financing for such an undertaking can not be encompassed by private effort but must be undertaken by the Government."[10]

[9] Black, *op. cit.,* note 5, pp. 342–343.
[10] *Economic Essays,* pp. 280–281. The Macmillan Company (1927).

In spite of statements put out by the United States Department of Agriculture, which officially has frequently inclined to the contrary view, Mr. Pope's persuasive survey of the evidence leads him to the conclusion that with wheat and cotton, "The much talked of congestion due to too rapid marketing is largely a myth in so far as the United States is concerned." Because of the size of the producing area and the variety of climatic conditions, harvesting of wheat begins in the South in June; it is still in full swing in the Northwest in September. The first of the season's cotton comes on the market in September; picking in the latest fields is not completed until February. So far as these crops are concerned it is Mr. Pope's judgment that "The real significance, therefore, of the demand for credit for holding for higher prices lies in the . . . proposition, *viz.*, that the working of the law of supply and demand does not bring about satisfactory prices and that what is sought [by the coöperative pools] is not the normal market price but something more, namely, a satisfactory price, or a fair price."

Coöperative marketing appears to work best in the case of fruits and vegetables, nuts, eggs, fluid milk and dairy products. The possibilities of coöperative buying by farmers, so as to effect economics in purchasing, are being rapidly explored but have not as yet been fully developed.

So far as the great farm staples, like corn, cotton and wheat, are concerned, the benefits to be derived from coöperative marketing (without a control over production) remain unconvincing.

In contrast with the orthodox administration program

of higher tariff duties on agricultural products and legislation to promote coöperative marketing, the leaders of the Farm Bloc, who felt that this program did not go far enough and was advanced partly to stall off more radical action, might have pursued two logical approaches. They might have insisted that industrial duties be lowered. In the view of economists generally, this would have been the sounder course. Instead, they directed their attention to proposals to make the tariff effective on agricultural staples.

The two schemes devised for this purpose were the equalization-fee and the export-debenture plans.

The last two McNary-Haugen bills, which were only stopped from becoming law by President Coolidge's veto, represent an evolution from bills which failed of passage in Congress in 1924, 1925 and 1926. We shall not attempt to analyze the features of all these different bills. Each was built around the principle of the equalization fee.

The export-debenture principle was embodied in bills introduced in Congress in 1926, 1928 and 1929. Because of the widespread ignorance of the real nature of these proposals, and the misconceptions which were stimulated by the various attacks made upon them, few realize how closely both were linked with the tariff issue. This relation appears when we grasp clearly the theory of the respective proposals.

After the failure of the stabilization operations of the Federal Farm Board both the equalization-fee and the export-debenture plans had active adherents. It is by no means certain that these plans are dead.

The following definitions, which are attributed to agricultural sources by the *National Sphere*, from which they are taken, have been chosen for their simplicity and clarity:

1. *Equalization Fee:*

Under this plan a Federal agency would collect a set fee, at the point of processing or transportation, on each marketed unit of a given commodity. It would be assessed on the entire crop sold, whether for domestic consumption or for export. The funds secured from the imposition of the fee would be used to finance the handling and selling abroad of the surplus. Thus the grower would finance the selling expense and the direct loss incident to disposal of the surplus in the world market.

2. *Export Debenture:*

The essential feature of the debenture plan is that certificates, known as debentures, negotiable in the payment of import on all products, would be issued on exports of farm products. The plan, as evolved, contemplates the issuance of debentures equal to 50 per cent of our import duties levied on each commodity. As a safeguard against increasing over-production the amount of the debenture would be reduced proportionately, as over-production of the commodity increased.[11]

Both plans are methods of making tariff duties effective on export farm staples. It is a truism that, no matter how high a tariff duty may be placed upon a farm product of which there is an exportable surplus, the duty is ineffective in influencing the price. In order to gain adherents from the cotton-growing states, provisions

[11] *The National Sphere,* Oct., 1931, p. 28.

in the alternative for cotton were included in the 1926 McNary-Haugen bill and in the bills vetoed by President Coolidge in 1927 and 1928. Although more than half of the Democratic representatives in the House and the Senate voted for the 1927 and the 1928 bills and the equalization-fee principle was vaguely (but very vaguely) endorsed by the party platform and the nominee in the 1928 national campaign, the McNary-Haugen plan was never entirely successful in silencing the opposition of old-line Democratic leaders, who saw in it a violation of fundamental Democratic principles. In 1926, for instance, it was denounced in the Senate by Senator Glass, as a Siamese twin of the protective tariff, a subsidy to agriculture just as industrial duties are a subsidy to manufacturing.

Under both the equalization-fee and the export-debenture plans, the maximum which the producer may receive is the world price plus the amount of the import duty and transportation costs. As a matter of fact, under the proposals in Congress this full maximum price would not be realized by the grower. If the McNary-Haugen plan were put in operation, the domestic prices would be raised to the extent that the surplus of the commodity was wholly or partially taken off the domestic market. The net realized by the grower would be this price, less the amount of the equalization fee. The export-debenture plan would aim to raise the price by one-half the import duty.

The essential differences of the two plans can be more easily understood by illustrations of how they would probably work in the case of a single export commodity, such as wheat. The McNary-Haugen plan would work out about as follows: At present there is an import duty of 42 cents on wheat. The domestic crop for the last five years has averaged well over 800,000,000 bushels; but let us assume an annual crop of 800,000,000 bushels, with export surplus of 200,000,000 bushels, to be sold abroad at a loss. If the world price is $1 and the entire surplus is taken off the domestic market, the price received by the American farmer for his crop would be increased by the full amount of the import duty to $1.42 plus transportation costs. Against this the grower would have to pay an equalization fee of 10½ cents, representing the loss on 200,000,000 bushels bought at $1.42 per bushel and sold abroad at $1, the loss of $84,000,000 being distributed over the entire crop. The net price realized by the American wheat grower thus would be $1.31½ per bushel. At an expense of $84,000,000 the growers would receive a clear gain of $252,000,000 on the entire crop.

We cannot enter into a discussion of the advantages of the plan urged by its proponents, or the objections which were raised to it in the two lengthy veto messages of President Coolidge, or in the opinion of Attorney-General Sargent annexed to the second veto message. Opponents have made much of its bureaucratic administrative features and its attempted price-fixing fallacy.

On the latter point, we might say able economists have taken the view that it is no more price-fixing than the tariff. For instance, Professor Black, whose support appears to have been based upon the strategy of the practical situation rather than upon a liking for the plan, was of the opinion that "the equalization plan is price-fixing in exactly the same way that the tariff is price-fixing. . . . It may be argued that whether prices are fixed absolutely or relative to a moving price is inconsequential—it is still price-fixing; but if so, import duties are price-fixing." [12] Sir Josiah Stamp, a leading English economist, in discussing the plan, said: "The scheme is not a price-fixing one, for it merely creates an addition to a moving world price."

One effect of the measure, of course, would be that it would raise the cost of living in this country. As Secretary Mellon pointed out in his official letter of June 25, 1926, it would not only raise the price of food products to the American consumer, but it would also cheapen their price to foreign consumers. This, of course, would operate to the disadvantage of American manufacturing, requiring higher wages to the American laborer and enabling the foreign laborer to live more cheaply than before. "Foreign industrial costs would be lowered and the foreign competitor assisted in underselling American products abroad and in our home market." This from the stronghold of protection! The argument, of course, is a dangerous one from the industrial point of view, for, conversely, high industrial duties penalize the American producer of farm staples, increasing his wage-bill and other costs and permitting low-cost countries like Canada, the Argentine and Australia to undersell him in the markets of the world.

On this point, *Bulletin 17* of the North Central States Conference says:

"If the Hoover-Mellon policy of expanding industrial exports, no matter at what costs to other groups, means anything at all, it means the definite submergence of agriculture. These

[12] Black, *op. cit.*, note 5, pp. 237–238.

men and their policies say, in substance, that American farmers must provide the food and raw materials for American industry and labor at prices no higher than foreign manufacturers and labor pay. Why? In order that American industry may export manufactured goods in competition with Europe." [13]

In contrast with McNary-Haugenism, the export-debenture plan is far simpler from an administrative viewpoint. An essential difference is that under the first the expenses of the disposal of the surplus crop would be financed by the farmers. Under the export-debenture plan they would come out of the receipts of the government from tariff duties. Because of this loss of revenues, the deficit would have to be met by increased federal taxation, either by raising the income and inheritance tax rates, or, as Congress might be more likely to do, by raising still higher existing import duties.

The export-debenture plan would operate about as follows: With the present tariff duty of 42 cents, exporters of wheat would receive a bounty from the government in the form of a customs-house certificate for 21 cents per bushel exported. This bounty would act as an inducement to the exporter to buy wheat in the United States up to a maximum of 21 cents more than the world price, but he would still be able to sell at the world price without suffering a loss on the transaction. If the world price were $1, he might be able to bid up to $1.21 in the domestic wheat market, though of course this figure is only a rough one, as differentials in freight and other costs would have to be considered. In order to simplify the illustration, we will assume, however, that the grower receives the full 21 cents addition to the world price of $1

[13] Quoted by Black, *op. cit.*, note 5, p. 248.

per bushel. Because of the fact that exporters will be able to bid 21 cents more per bushel of wheat, it may reasonably be assumed that the surplus crop will be entirely exported and that domestic consumers will be forced to bid 21 cents more per bushel for the balance of the crop which is consumed in this country. With an 800,000,000 bushel wheat crop, the growers will thus receive $168,-000,000 more than they would have gotten without the 21 cent debenture, but the actual cost of the debenture to the government will be based only on the 200,000,000 bushels exported, and the actual loss to the government in customs-receipts would be $42,000,000.

Those who favor the export-debenture plan claim that it was first suggested by Alexander Hamilton as a part of the original tariff system of the United States. Wilson Gee, in *The Place of Agriculture in American Life,* comments:

"This financial genius [Hamilton] to whom the protection policy of this country owes so much is said to have pointed out that if the tariff policy was adopted with regard to manufacturers, Congress should also adopt the export premium policy in order that agriculture should not be discriminated against and thereby injured. Congress adopted the tariff on manufactures, but failed to incorporate the suggestion of Hamilton, and we have today the proof of the correctness of his opinion, that the tariff would benefit the manufacturer more than the farmer." [14]

It is not generally realized by the farmers that under our present tariff laws American manufacturers are refunded the duties, less one per cent, paid on foreign raw materials used in exported manufactures, upon a sworn

[14] Gee, *The Place of Agriculture in American Life,* pp. 170–171. The Macmillan Company (1930).

affidavit of the exporter as proof of such use. This practice, while not entirely analogous to the export-debenture, affords another illustration of how the tariff system has been framed primarily to suit the requirements of industry.

Although a candid analysis of the literature of the subject justifies the opinion that in many respects neither the equalization-fee nor the export-debenture plan is more economically unsound than high protection is under existing world conditions, the equalization-fee and export-debenture plans are subject to damaging criticism on the grounds that (1) the increase in production which will follow from the stimulation of higher prices, will lower the world price, and (2) the interests of the country will be injured by foreign retaliations.

Authorities agree that the export-debenture plan, in particular, would be a strong stimulus to increased production of the crops to which it was made applicable. Realizing this danger, the authors of the legislation proposed that the amount of the export bounty should be decreased from time to time or canceled altogether if necessary to curb too great increases in production. Because the effectiveness of this safeguard would depend upon forecasts, as to which human judgment has proven in the past highly fallible, and upon its successful employment by a federal board, against which powerful political pressure would be exerted to prevent the debentures being decreased at the right time, its efficacy to accomplish its purpose would seem questionable.

No less serious is the danger of foreign reprisals. When, in order to establish foreign credits with which to buy machinery needed to carry out the Five-Year Plan, Russia sold wheat on the world markets, it was called dumping. The Russian practice aroused a great hullabaloo in other countries in the fall of 1930. The equalization-fee and the export-debenture plans, because the central idea of each is the disposal abroad of our own surplus, for whatever it will bring, on the world markets, would lay the United States open to the same charge of dumping. Foreign workmen and the general mass of people in foreign countries would benefit from getting food more cheaply; but foreign governments could hardly be expected to withstand inevitable pressure from their own agricultural interests to increase the import duties and restrictions on American products. As is well known, protected industry, unable to sell within the walls of the American protective system the entire output of mass-production, sometimes found it good business, in order to avoid glutting the American market, to sell its surplus production abroad for less than the American price. This practice was one of the factors which caused foreign countries to vie with each other in putting up tariff barriers against imports of American manufactures. The equalization-fee and export-debenture plans, which were designed to give government assistance to agriculture in order that it may do the same thing, would undoubtedly provoke a similar reaction abroad.

The danger of foreign retaliations is probably greater in the case of the export-debenture plan because, as Professor Black, a sympathetic critic, points out, the specific rates of the debentures "would tend to be the exact amounts which would be added to the import duties" abroad. The same thing would be likely to happen abroad that happened in the United States when, as of January 1,

1929, the Australian government put a bounty of nine cents per pound on the export of Australian butter. Promptly the Secretary of the Treasury at Washington, acting under authority created by the Fordney-McCumber Tariff Act, instructed the Collectors of the Customs to impose an additional duty on Australian butter equivalent to the increase in the Australian bounty.

To sum up, both the equalization-fee and the export-debenture plans would stimulate production. But industrial import duties do also. Both the equalization-fee and the export-debenture plans, invoking as they do governmental aid for surplus-disposal abroad, would invite foreign reprisals. The practice of some American mass-producers, of dumping their surplus production abroad, without government aid, invites the same thing. Except for their objectionable bureaucratic features, the equalization-fee and the export-debenture plans are not necessarily more unsound economically than high industrial duties are under existing world conditions.

An important objection to the adoption of either the equalization-fee or export-debenture plan is that such adoption would furnish entrench a system of high industrial import duties at a time when, in spite of a decade of unabashed economic nationalism, the longer national interest calls for a lowering of high protective tariffs throughout the world.

In 1928 both political parties bid for the farm vote by promising to enact into law a program that would solve the problems of the farmer. The election of President Hoover cleared the way for the adoption of the Hoover brand of relief. This comprised two principal features, (1) higher tariff on agricultural imports and (2) the creation of a Federal Farm Board to grant assistance in the marketing of farm products (in the words of the Republican nominee) "on sounder and more stable and more economic lines," and to "protect the farmer from the depressions and demoralizations of seasonal gluts and periodical surpluses." [15]

The first point in this program was achieved with the passage of the Hawley-Smoot Tariff Bill; the second, with the enactment of the Agricultural Marketing Act. It is to the latter and to the work of the Federal Farm Board that we shall devote the balance of this chapter.

The bright hopes that were held out by the Republican nominee for the Farm Board experiment make melancholy reading at the present time. Like his confident prediction that "we shall soon, with the help of God, be in sight of the day when poverty will be banished from this nation," they were vitiated by an irrational psychology that prevailed during the Wall Street boom. It seems almost unkind to recall that in his acceptance speech at Palo Alto, Mr. Hoover, in proposing the establishment of the Farm Board, announced that it was to "establish for our farmers an income equal to those of other occupations; for the farmer's wife the same comforts in her home as women in other groups; for the farm boys and girls the same opportunities in life as other boys and girls."

The blasting of this illusion may be measured by the fact that prior to the creation of the Federal Farm Board in July, 1929, cotton was selling at $100 a bale and wheat at $1.65 a bushel. These prices were considered

[15] Acceptance Speech at Palo Alto, California (1928).

so low that the Agricultural Marketing Act was rushed through Congress to meet what was considered at the time an agricultural crisis. In July, 1931, wheat was selling for 50 cents a bushel, and cotton for around $30.00 a bale. Although the operations of the Farm Board were futile to stay the decline except for temporary periods, all fair-minded persons must, however, recognize that in passing judgment on the principles of the Agricultural Marketing Act, allowance must be made for the collapse of commodity prices all over the world during the same period.

The Board began its work under two severe handicaps which were scarcely appreciated at the time. In the first place, it was faced with the impossibility of living up to the extravagant expectations which had been aroused by its political propagandists. The opening paragraph from an article by Charles W. Holman in the *World's Work* of October, 1929, may bring back the unreal psychology which had been created:

"Since last July millions of farm people have been deliberating whether to have water piped into the house, buy a new stove, or pay off the mortgage as soon as the Farm Relief Board started work. When Congress passed the Agricultural Marketing Act, the farmers immediately pinned their hopes on the price-raising powers of the government. Few were familiar with the details of the new law, but in a general way all had known for six or seven years that Congress was wrestling with the problem of farm relief. It was natural that they should expect increased prices of farm products. . . ."

In the second place, a hardly less auspicious time could have been chosen to launch a daring experiment to control the free play of economic forces than the summer of 1929. Already, general business had begun to decline and the speculative collapse of October, 1929, was only a few months off. Yet in those warm summer days of 1929, with the stock market soaring to new and unheard of heights, there were few who had an inkling that the world was on the brink of the worst economic crisis of modern times. In the desire to find a universal scape-goat, unsympathetic critics failed to mention these forgotten circumstances.

With respect to the membership of the Board, a number had had wide experience in coöperative marketing. All but two of the eight original appointees had been closely associated with agricultural coöperative enterprises. All, even Mr. Legge, who gave up a salary of $100,000 a year with the International Harvester Company, if not actual farmers, had had a background of farm environment.

The truth is, the Board was faced with a task of herculean proportions that was to prove impossible of realization within the framework of the Act.

In his address to the assembled Board in the White House offices on July 15, 1929, President Hoover said:

> "I invest you with responsibilities and resources such as have never before been conferred by our Government in assistance to any industry."

For the purposes of the experiment, Congress appropriated a revolving fund of $500,000,000. The Act itself contained a congeries of objectives. The two which bulked largest in the activities of the Board were (1) the organization of producers into associations for the coöperative marketing of each major farm product and the financing of their activities, and (2) the prevention and control of agricultural surpluses.

To achieve the first objective, the Board at once directed its attention to the integration of existing agricultural coöperatives, and under its direction federated organizations were formed, operating over entire sections in livestock, wheat, cotton and various commodities. The formation of these central marketing agencies has been under fire, and the full story of their activities is yet to be told. Because of the policy which the Board followed of not loaning except to coöperatives, it was attacked not only by established grain dealers who saw their business faced with extinction, but also by independent producers not affiliated with coöperatives.

The program which the Board adopted to accomplish the second objective, subjected it to even more criticism. The Board early interpreted the Agricultural Marketing Act to mean that, in addition to financing coöperatives to buy crops and store them, or to make crop loans to farmers, it should organize so-called stabilization corporations to buy commodities from coöperatives when the latter were not themselves able to carry the crops.

Although President Hoover, in his message to the extra session of Congress in 1929, had stated: "No government agency should engage in buying and selling and price-fixing of products, for such courses can lead only to bureaucracy and domination," it is inconceivable that the Board's stabilization activities did not have the full support of the administration, in spite of the President's disclaimer, on at least one occasion, of responsibility for its decisions.

In considering the stabilization corporations which were organized under direction of the Board, it is necessary to observe that, within narrow limits and with favoring conditions, the principle behind them is workable. The condition of success would seem to be that a large crop be followed by a short world crop. As *The New Republic* observed in its issue of December 9, 1931:

"The basic theory of stabilization is simple. . . . If prices are temporarily low through an abnormally large crop *which is not likely soon to be duplicated,* it would be possible, by buying and holding off the market enough of the crop, to sustain prices. Then the holdings might be sold without loss at a future period when supply was smaller in relation to demand. This remedy would be effective in smoothing out price variations due to weather conditions and varying yields. But if the price difficulty is caused by *persistent over-production* in relation to demand, stabilization is worse than useless. Either it temporarily succeeds in maintaining prices, in which case it encourages more production and thus makes the eventual crash worse, or it does not succeed in maintaining prices, and thus throws money down a bottomless hole."

Further, if enough money is available to buy the entire exportable surplus in any one commodity, so that the duty on foreign importations can be made effective, it is theoretically possible artificially to raise the price which the grower in this country may receive, by the amount of the import duty, whatever that may be.

The clear effect of the combination of these two factors—Farm Board purchases, plus the import duty—may be seen from the fact that at the end of November, 1930, there was a differential of sixteen to eighteen cents between the price of wheat in Chicago and the price in Winnipeg across the border. During most of the first half of 1931, artificial prices for cash wheat and all future deliveries up to May 31 were maintained by the Board. The cessation of stabilization purchases under Chairman Stone, who had succeeded Chairman Legge early in 1931, was followed by a decline of prices, and with a large new crop impending, the prices in Chicago of nearby deliveries fell by the middle of August approximately twenty-five cents per bushel.

None of the Farm Board's stabilization operations in wheat and cotton succeeded, except for temporary periods, of which the above is the most important, in stemming the collapse of prices which continued as part of the economic phenomena of the world-wide crisis. The Board's purchases in wheat and cotton may be divided into three periods—two in wheat and one in cotton. Judging from externals only, each of these bears evidence of having been embarked upon under the urgency of circumstances.

The mistakes of the Board appear to have been typical business men's mistakes of judgment. A grave one was made at the time of the Wall Street collapse in October, 1929. Along with the rest of the administration and outstanding leaders in the industrial and banking world, the Board appears to have failed to grasp that an era had come to an end. The story is told as follows by Charles Merz, special reporter for *The New York Times* in *The Times* of July 26, 1931:

"Declaring that the current prices of wheat and cotton were too low, the board announced its readiness to loan to cotton coöperatives on their holdings at an average of 16 cents a pound and to wheat coöperatives on their holdings at $1.18 a bushel in Chicago and $1.25 in Minneapolis.

"This move was necessarily a gamble, since cotton and wheat were then selling at approximately these prices in the open market and the board was making loans up to 100 per cent in value. If prices had risen after this announcement, the board would doubtless have won great prestige for the accuracy with which it picked the bottom of the market. Unfortunately, prices declined, particularly the price of wheat. In October, 1929, wheat for near delivery was selling in Chicago for $1.21. By February, 1930, it reached a new low of 98¾ cents. During much of this period the board was loaning to coöperatives from 5 to 20 cents more per bushel than wheat was worth in the market. The coöperatives could not sell their wheat for enough to repay their loans.

"In these circumstances the Farm Board found it necessary to set up a Grain Stabilization Corporation, with an initial loan of $10,000,000, to buy wheat from the coöperatives at the price at which it had loaned its funds. It was now in the business of buying grain. Meantime it also attempted to support the market by purchasing cash wheat at market prices and by purchasing May futures. In this policy it apparently had the support of the administration, despite the President's earlier statement that 'no governmental agency should engage in the buying and selling' of farm products. The action of the board in buying wheat was extended shortly to the buying of cotton."

In other words, through an initial misjudgment of the future prospects of the market and to rescue the cooperatives, to which it had made loans, from serious trouble, the Board seems to have gotten into the grain pit by the back door. According to statements which appeared in the press, the Board purchased, during the 1929–1930 crop season, approximately 70,000,000 bushels of wheat at an estimated average price of $1.18 a bushel, and 1,300,000 bales of cotton at an average price of 16 cents a pound or $80 a bale.

With the continuing decline of prices, purchases of both wheat and cotton were discontinued, and in the summer of 1930 the Board indicated pretty clearly that it was through with stabilization—that is, unless further emergencies should arise. On August 25, 1930, Mr. Legge, then Chairman of the Board, went into the reasons why "the proposal to buy 100 million bushels of wheat, although it might raise prices temporarily, would intensify some of the effects of the wheat surplus without leading to any real solution." As a writer in *The New Republic* of April 15, 1931, summarized this address:

> "He pointed out, . . . that such a purchase would accelerate movement of wheat from farms; it would cut down exports during the cream of our export seasons; it would increase terminal congestion and the price spread between farm and terminal; it would not permanently raise the level of wheat prices; it would discriminate against farmers who had already sold."

Nevertheless, the threatening situation in November, 1930, caused the Board to lay aside scruples such as these and enter upon a second period of wheat stabilization. With unusually optimistic crop reports from the Argentine and an exportable surplus from Russia estimated at 110,000,000 bushels, Canadian banks were asking for increased margins from the Canadian wheat pool, a monster farmers' organization that had also been withholding wheat from the world markets and was deeply in debt to the banks for loans on its holdings. The domestic situation had become serious likewise, as explained thus by Chairman Stone in his 1931 Annual Report:

> "In mid-November many important banks failed in agricultural States. Further declines in prices appeared likely to bankrupt many coöperatives and to cause a general financial collapse.
>
> "If a heavy movement to market had resulted from forced liquidation of wheat, enormous discounts for cash wheat would have followed. Lenders of every sort had made advances on grain. The general economic situation is a very delicate one and might react violently to further declines in the price of one of the great agricultural staples. Banking and mercantile credit throughout the wheat belt was conditioned to a considerable extent on wheat prices. The emergency was acute and involved all wheat farmers, directly or indirectly.

"The sharp break in world prices and the further declines which seemed in prospect thus convinced the board that an emergency existed which could be met only by increased stabilization purchases."

At the Farm Board hearings in November, 1931, Mr. Stone testified that if the price of wheat had dropped two cents, the whole financial structure of the country might have been endangered.

Between November 17, 1930 and May 31, 1931, when, as already mentioned, the Board stopped stabilization purchases of the grain, it acquired enough additional wheat to bring its total purchases up to over 329,000,000 bushels.

After the cessation of stabilization purchases the Board's most important task was to dispose of its holdings with as little loss and disturbance to the market as possible. At no time was there an opportunity to do this at a profit; and likewise pressure was exerted by leaders of the agricultural bloc in Congress to restrict sales, because of the opposition of farmers trying to sell while the Board was selling. Under such pressure in June, 1930, the Board was constrained to announce that it would limit its sales of stabilizing wheat to a cumulative maximum of 5,000,000 bushels a month.

This rapid survey of the activities of the Board necessarily touches only the high spots in the record. Sufficient time has, however, elapsed to permit certain conclusions. As Chairman Stone admitted in his 1931 Annual Report, "it is futile to engage in stabilization purchases for any product over a period of years in the face of a constantly accumulating surplus of that product." Others see in its experience the weakness of price stabilization as a method of farm relief. Merely *withholding* from the market the surplus production of a farm staple like wheat or cotton will not prevent prices falling with the *contraction* of export demand. Prices are depressed because the wheat trade knows that the withheld surplus must eventually be sold. The very uncertainty created by ignorance as to when it may come on the market tends to unsettle the world price. The Board, on the other hand, has to decide whether the sale of wheat will do more damage to prevailing prices than continuing to hold it as a threat over the market will do. The longer it waits for higher prices, the higher the price must be if it is to break even. This is because carrying charges, including not only the usual warehouse charges but loss of interest on capital tied up in the commodity, pile up the longer it waits.

So far as the Board is concerned, it labored valiantly and with the best of intentions to carry out the wishes of the President and the acknowledged intent and purpose of the Agricultural Marketing Act. Within narrow limitations this program might have worked in less abnormal times. Under the conditions which prevailed after 1929, no Board could have made "stabilization" a success. Needless to say, it did not deserve the torrent of criticism to which it was subjected. Much of this was inconsistent. Said Jay Franklin in *The Forum Magazine* of February, 1932:

> "It is doubtful that any government agency has ever been attacked for so many and so contradictory reasons as the Farm Board. It was attacked for not buying wheat when prices began to drop. Five Farm Bloc Senators begged Chairman Legge as early as 1929 to use the revolving fund to keep the price above a dollar. Then the Board was attacked for possessing the wheat which it had bought. The existence of the mere 200,-

000,000 bushels which the farmers had unloaded on the Board depressed the market. Julius Barnes attacked the Board for favoring the coöperatives on almost the same day that Senator Caraway attacked the Board for favoring the private speculators as against the coöperatives. The Chicago Board of Trade solemnly proposed repealing the Act, and the U. S. Chamber of Commerce disapproved of using government money to help the coöperatives.

"When the Board traded wheat for coffee with the Brazilian Government, the action was attacked by the farmers, the coffee dealers, and the American shipping men whose rates were too high to carry the goods economically. Proposals to sell wheat to China, France, and Germany, cotton to France and Germany, were all attacked. Senator Capper begged the Board to hold its wheat off the market until the price reached 90 cents a bushel, although it was costing the Board $4,000,000 a month to carry it, and then the Board was attacked for cutting down carrying charges by having some of the wheat turned into flour. . . . The Board has a high scapegoat value."

A more serious criticism is the loss of government moneys resulting from the Board's stabilization operations. The *actual* loss, of course, cannot be determined until all the accounts are finally liquidated. The new Farm Credits Administration has estimated that it will be around $360,000,000. While this amount seems staggering, it is but about sixty millions more than the Fordney-McCumber Tariff Act of 1922 was estimated to cost the farmers in *one year.* In 1923 the American Farm Bureau, after investigations and a study carried on by its research department, estimated that the net cost of the latter to the farmers of the country was $301,000,000 *a year.* This net loss was arrived at after deducting $30,000,000, representing the gain which it was estimated accrued to the farmers a year from effective tariff duties on agricultural imports provided for in the

Act. These figures of the American Farm Bureau have not, so far as the author is aware, been challenged.

The Farm Board's activities were spread over nearly four years. If we multiply by four the farmers' net loss from the Fordney-McCumber Tariff we get $1,204,-000,000, a figure that dwarfs the Farm Board's estimated loss of $360,000,000.

The comparison of these figures should be kept in mind by those who object to the farmers becoming the special pet of the federal government.

A decade or more of farm relief may be summed up in the statement that America refused to face the fundamentals of the situation. The failure of the Farm Board's stabilization operations has confirmed the farmer's own deep-seated skepticism as to the ability of the government to do anything really effective about the essential problem, which is how to place the farmers on an economic equality with other classes of the population.

There are two ways, as we have already mentioned, in which the inequality of the farmers may be lessened. One way is through special subsidies to match the tariff subsidy to industry. The Farm Bloc, in its long fight for the equalization-fee or export debenture plans, followed this logical approach. Although the risks of schemes such as these are great and no one can precisely predict how they will work until they are tried, they attack fundamentals more directly than ineffective stabilization operations in wheat and cotton.

The other, believed by most economists to be the sounder way, is by the gradual withdrawal of tariff privileges that unduly favor industry.

This lesson we failed to learn during a decade which must be characterized as a decade of frustration. It was necessary for the world depression to make clear the anatomy of our economic structure.

CHAPTER V

AMERICA AT THE CROSSROADS

In *The Epic of America,* James Truslow Adams took the view that it is a national characteristic for the people of the United States to run away from the solution of national difficulties. This is due, he believes, to the circumstance that, until the turn of the last century, after every severe business depression, the vast tracts of unsettled territory furnished a haven for the jobless, the propertyless and the disaffected generally. A man, no matter how low he might fall in the economic scale, could always get a new start by going West. There, at least, he could receive from the hands of the government a quarter-section of land upon which he might build a home of his own. Then, too, since the disappearance of the frontier, we have been engrossed in the exploitation of the natural resources of the continent and the development of the technique of mass-production, a task which has absorbed the energies and ambitions of the people, without affording the opportunity for thought as to whither we were heading. So, thinks Mr. Adams, an inclination has arisen for "slipping out from under a situation, when it becomes too complex, rather than thinking and fighting it through," which has grown into a national trait.

The farm problem is one instance in support of this thesis.

As long ago as 1908, the late Theodore Roosevelt observed: "The farmer is, as a rule, better off than his forbears, but his increase in well-being has not kept pace with that of the country at large."

We have already indicated how the roots of the present agricultural crisis go back much further than the days of the elder Roosevelt. They are embedded deep in American history.

One reason why it has taken the people so long to get at the bottom of the question has been the ineffectiveness of farm leadership in contrast with that of industry. On the one hand, the huge rewards which industry has offered to those who desired to rise to places of great wealth or of great power over the affairs of their fellowmen have acted as a magnet to draw to the service of industry the ablest brains of the nation. On the other hand, there have been few with the capacity or the training to present the farmer's case in a way effectively to command attention from the nation at large, and theirs has mostly been a thankless job.

During the past decade, city-dwellers, for the most part, were unaware that there was a farm problem.

This illusion no longer exists. Not only do thinking men now generally appreciate that agriculture led the way downwards into the depths of the depression, but they seriously question whether capitalism and the American government, in the form in which it has been handed down by the forefathers, can long endure without the restoration of the lost balance between the conflicting, yet interdependent, interests of the farm and of the factory.

The bane of the industrial age is unemployment. There is no question that unemployment will continue one of our greatest problems for a considerable time in the future, regardless of how soon we get out of the trough of the depression. Looking ahead over a period of years, one may safely predict an accentuation of class consciousness and a sharpening of the lines between capital and labor.

The principal basis making for the continued social and political stability of the nation is the existence of a middle group whose interests coincide neither with those of modern capitalism nor of unionist labor. In this group the farmers constitute the largest single element. As a class, they constitute the mainstay of American individualism opposed to radicalism fashioned along either Fascistist or communist lines. It may well be that, because he is a capitalist himself in a small way, and therefore unalterably opposed to the surrender of his individual rights either to a socialistic state or to anyone else, the old-fashioned individual farmer is, as one recent writer has remarked, "not only the mainstay of capitalism, but probably its last bulwark." [1]

If this be so, it would seem, if we are to avoid fundamental changes in our form of government and in the system of American property rights, that the industrialists should make the farmers the object of their special concern.

To restore the lost balance which has developed between farming and industry, it is not necessary that industry should be maimed, but there should be withdrawn

[1] Dennis, *Is Capitalism Doomed?* p. 145. Harper & Brothers (1932).

from it the false stimulants which have produced an elephantiasis, while subtracting nourishment from other parts of the economic organism. In this way the interests of the nation can best be subserved.

Little Alice has developed abnormally. Her head and hands have grown too large for the rest of her body. What she needs is neither a surgical operation that will attempt to lop off the overgrown parts, nor pink patent-medicine pills, but a regimen of living that will tend to develop the weakened organs. Besides, her glands are out of shape. They are not functioning, and her circulatory system is in danger of atrophy.

In the present chapter we shall attempt to examine the farm problem in the setting of its relation to the system of policies toward the rest of the world, which our government has pursued in the years since the War.

It is the particular vice of most plans for the solution of the farm problem that, while often logically presented and well-organized, they either ignore the fundamental causes of the farmers' difficulties, or else fail to take into account adequately the world context within which definitive, as opposed to temporary, solutions must be found.

We shall discuss later the unfolding of the Roosevelt farm program. We shall also discuss later such matters as taxation, land policies and the like, which are more readily isolated as parts of the purely domestic picture.

The well-being of agriculture is intimately related to the fortunes of other businesses and of other nations.

In the years of drift after the World War the United

States failed squarely to face the peculiar problems which have devolved upon her as a result of the War. We continued to blind ourselves to the responsibilities thrust upon us by the change of our debtor-creditor relationship with the rest of the world. Economists generally recognize that our tariff, debt and foreign policies over most of the past decade were antagonistic to this changed relationship. If Washington and Wall Street should succeed in "slipping out from under" the present situation without "thinking and fighting it through," we may recover from the present depression, but there can be no assurance that the next one will not be even more devastating in its consequences. Continued temporizing threatens final irreparable disaster to our industries, our institutions and our individual liberties.

Before the War the problem of private international debt payments presented no particular difficulties. The United States was a debtor nation, paying its debts to Europe largely in American farm products. The great creditor nations of the pre-war world had, generally speaking, supplied capital and credit to the other nations in order that the latter might establish transportation systems and expand their power to produce commodities of which the creditor nations were in need.

The wealth and prosperity of Great Britain illustrated the benefits which a creditor nation might enjoy by pursuing policies consistent with her creditor position. Not only did Great Britain interpose no obstacles to imports of every kind, but she created markets for practically everything which the world produced, thus assisting the nations to which she had supplied credit and capital to meet their obligations.

The consequences were an immense expansion in the world's productive power, wealth, income and trade, and with it a corresponding growth in those of Great Britain.

The United States, on the other hand, has followed different policies. From a creditor nation at the outbreak of hostilities in 1914, to the extent of approximately three billions of dollars net, the United States has changed to a long-term creditor of the rest of the world to the extent of nearly twenty-seven billions of dollars. The War created an immense foreign demand for the products of our farms, mines and factories. By the extension of almost unlimited credits we were able to sell to Europe our wheat, cotton, tobacco, meats and meat products, munitions, steel, copper and a host of other commodities, at extremely profitable prices. We took in exchange promises to pay. By a continuance of credits, this interchange continued for a while after the Armistice. Our prosperity during and after the War was based upon loans to, and the continuance of the abnormal demand for our products from, nations whose producing effectiveness had been laid low by the ravages of the War.

What we did not realize then is that a people cannot go on indefinitely extending credits without regard for how they are to be repaid. Allowing credits to pile up, without a thought as to how they are to be repaid, merely delays the day of settlement, making it worse in the end.

A curious delusion prevailed that we could go on selling our products abroad, simply by extending more credit.

A collapse came in 1920, when foreign collections slowed up and our bankers shut off for a while the supply of new credit, but the lesson which Washington and

Wall Street should have learned then was unheeded, and our people failed even to appreciate its significance.

Among them, an equally curious delusion prevailed that it would be possible for our foreign debtors to pay us and at the same time continue to buy from us the products they would need from us under normal conditions, without our allowing them freely to sell us goods in exchange.

If we had followed the example of Great Britain and the other great creditor nations of Europe before the War, we would have facilitated the payment by our debtors of the interest and amortization charges on their debts by lowering our tariff or adopting free trade. Instead of recognizing that our change from a debtor to a creditor of the rest of the world called for a change in our protective tariff policy, we increased the tariff in 1922 and again in 1930.

In spite of the industrial boom which was kept going by an inflation of bank credit, thus financing instalment buying at home and a flow of loans to foreign countries, there existed throughout the decade a peculiar international financial tension which was the result of the inconsistent foreign investment and trade policy situation which we have in part described.

According to the United States Department of Commerce, there accrues annually on the long-term debts which the rest of the world owes us, either to private American investors or to the United States Government, approximately $1,380,000,000.[2]

One learns from elementary economic texts that this yearly sum can be paid in one of three ways. These are

[2] *Trade Information Bulletin No. 761*, p. 39. U. S. Dept. of Comm.

(1) by shipments to us of gold; (2) by selling us goods and services; and (3) by selling us securities, or, in other words, by our extending further capital and credit.

As Professor Alvin Harvey Hansen remarks in his *Economic Stabilization in an Unbalanced World,* "all three methods have in fact been used" during the past decade:

"The first method, however, has intensified the maldistribution of the world's gold; the second has been made difficult by the American tariff policy; the third indeed lessened the tension up to 1929, but the present and prospective financial status of foreign governments, the political unrest, and world-wide depression, do not give any confidence that for some years to come foreign securities can or will be sold in the United States in sufficient volume to afford adequate relief. Thus a strain of increasing intensity has developed that is partly responsible for the breakdown of the world economic structure in 1929–30 and which threatens the continued prosperity not only of the United States but of the whole world." [3]

Another economist, Dr. B. M. Anderson, Jr., of The Chase National Bank of the City of New York, describes the situation thus:

"I like to use a homely figure of speech in describing our foreign investment and trade policy situation. The debts of the outside world to us are ropes about their necks, by means of which we pull them toward us. Our trade restrictions are pitchforks pressed against their bodies, by means of which we hold them off. The situation can obviously involve a very painful strain for the foreign debtor. But for the period from the middle of 1924 to the middle of 1928, we steadily eased the strain by feeding out more rope. Then, in the second half of 1928, what rope we did feed out we fed out painfully and slowly. We ceased to lend very much to the outside world." [4]

[3] Hansen, *Economic Stabilization in an Unbalanced World,* pp. 78–79. Harcourt, Brace and Company (1932).

[4] Quoted by Hansen, *op. cit.,* note 3, p. 79.

One reason for the severity of the crisis is that, by shutting out foreign manufactures, we exclude the very medium in which our principal European debtors, because of the nature of things, must pay their debts. The industrial part of Europe has insufficient arable land upon which to support its population. It is deficient in raw materials. Compared with parts of America the land is poor and its fertility has been depleted by centuries of cultivation. The greater part of the continent is situated between the same degrees of latitude as the region between Labrador and Maine in North America. In consequence the seasons for cultivation are shorter than in the United States, although the temperature is warmed by the Gulf Stream. In order to buy food and raw materials, industrial Europe has to make payment in finished products. With these barred out by the American tariff, Europe is forced to so-called "triangular" or "multi-angular" trade in order to meet her payments to America. In other words, she must sell finished goods in large quantities to the countries from which we draw raw materials such as rubber, coffee, copper, nitrates, etc., to acquire the necessary foreign exchange in order to meet her payments to America.

Another reason for the crisis is that during the years when we were lending freely abroad we were, at the same time, attempting aggressively to expand our exports of manufactures. Not only were the activities of the Department of Commerce pointed in this direction, but, with the public speculatively inclined, our mass-production industries were able to raise huge sums with which to expand their plants to handle a world market. In spite of the higher level of costs in the United States, industries such as the automobile industry and others were able to undersell competitors in foreign countries by economies in mass-production. Foreign lending was freely resorted to as a method of financing our expanded exports of finished goods, although the effect of such exports was to increase the difficulties of our principal debtors in industrial Europe to meet their payments to us, unless they borrowed from us the additional money with which to do so.

The contradictory policies which we have mentioned have been described by Walter Lippmann "as a composite of folly." "For," says he, "having by our tariff policy closed the American market to Europeans, having decided to thrust our exports into their markets, having determined to compete aggressively against them in the neutral markets of Latin America and of Asia, there were no ways by which they could balance their accounts with us except by sending us their gold and by borrowing from us." [5]

During the four years 1921–1924, nearly $1,500,000,000 net gold was imported into the United States. From then up until the middle of 1928 the movement was negligible, because we were meeting the abnormal situation by lavish foreign lending. During those years, as Dr. Anderson would say, we let out more rope. When foreign lending ceased in 1928, we began to take gold again from all parts of the world. Between June, 1928, and September 16, 1931, our gold holdings rose from $4,100,000,000 to over $5,000,000,000. After England

[5] Lippmann, "A Reckoning, Twelve Years of Republican Rule," reprinted from *The Yale Review,* Summer 1932, p. 652, by permission of the Editors.

and various other European nations were forced off the gold standard in the fall of 1931, there was a spectacular outflow of the yellow metal because the central banks of France and the other leading gold countries, threatened by a run on their own gold reserves, were busily engaged in calling home their foreign balances. While between September, 1931, and the middle of June, 1932, over $1,100,000,000 of gold flowed out of the United States, these exports were primarily the result of the determination of the remaining gold countries of Europe to stay on a gold basis; and over the long run, as opposed to the short run, the permanent forces based upon our changed status from a debtor to a great creditor nation, combined with our high-tariff policy, tended to drain the rest of the world of gold.

They were responsible, in part, for the breakdown of the international gold standard and the depreciation of foreign currencies. The world is not suffering at the present time from an insufficiency of gold, but from its maldistribution.

One effect of this maldistribution is to widen the differential between the price level in the United States and that in foreign countries, with an unwholesome effect in each.

A wide differential between the price level in the United States and that in foreign countries restricts the export of American farm products.

Professor Hansen explains the matter as follows:

"The American tariff policy by drawing gold from the rest of the world has had the effect of placing the trade and production of the outside world in the deadly grip of credit contraction, and thus forcing the world commodity price level steadily downward. This is one of the causes contributing to the world depression of 1930. Under the pressure of credit contraction and falling prices the outside world was unable to buy the usual quantity of American exports. . . .

"The wider the differential between American and world prices becomes, the more difficult it will be for American exporters to sell their goods in the world market. With prices higher in the United States than abroad, costs will also be higher. With lower prices in the industrial nations of Europe, their costs will also be lower. American exporters with their high costs will find it increasingly difficult to meet the competition in foreign lower-price markets. This is the two-edged sword of a high tariff policy.

"With the same stroke that the tariff cuts off imports, it also in the end cuts off exports. The day of reckoning may be postponed for a long time by means of foreign loans, as in the past decade. But the larger the loans become, the more inevitable the day of judgment. You cannot have your cake and eat it too, as they mistakenly believe who on the one hand seek to foster an export program, and on the other, seek to build a high tariff wall." [6]

No less disastrous for our exports is the absence of a stable international monetary standard. With violent fluctuations in the rate of exchange between currencies, importers and exporters dare not make commitments because they cannot tell what their goods will be worth upon delivery.

The crisis in American agriculture, which, in the author's view is due, more than to anything else, to lowered foreign demand for our exports of such farm staples as cotton, wheat, tobacco, pork and pork products, etc., naturally raises the question: What shall we do about it?

From those who appear to accept a high tariff as the settled policy of the country we get a variety of sug-

[6] Hansen, *op. cit.*, note 3, pp. 82–83.

gestions, none of which is completely satisfactory. These may be divided into two groups,—those that do not call for political action, and those that do.

The suggestions in the first group involve the question, What should the individual farmer do? Following are six characteristic answers, with their rationale briefly stated:

1. A suggestion frequently encountered is that based on the assumption that the farmer's chief difficulties arise from his increase in efficiency. The thing for him to do, therefore, is to aim at greater self-sufficiency and not seek to improve his efficiency by going in for specialized production and exchange. In other words, he should not seek to become a business man. Instead, he should be content with farming for subsistence rather than for profit.

Whatever may be the validity of the assumption (and as we have indicated in the first chapter, it can be supported by persuasive reasoning), the proposal has a certain appeal to hard common sense. It is one way in which the farmer can maintain a degree of independence of a world that is not run either to his liking or for his gain. Provided he can keep out of debt by buying few things from industry and work hard enough to grow sufficient to provide the wherewithal to pay his taxes and the few necessaries which he cannot produce himself, he can dispense with the expensive labor-saving machinery which is used in modern commercialized agriculture. Carried to a logical absurdity, the proposal involves a return to the age of homespun, the grist-mill, the home-made tallow-candle and lye soap cooked in an iron kettle. From the standpoint of the farmer, the fly in the ointment is that it means a lowered standard of living and a renunciation of the very human desire to keep up with his city cousin. From the standpoint of industry, it means that industry will lose a market for its products which in the aggregate is vastly important to scores of our nation-wide corporations.

2. Directly contradictory in spirit is the proposal that the salvation of the individual farmer is to apply to farming the type of organization and the methods which have been exploited and over-developed by industry. In other words, he should go in for the corporate farm type of organization which exercises a centralized control over output and employs the latest and most efficient means of mass-production of farm products. This idea, needless to say, is one that goes "big" with those who have acquired the habits of thought of big business. It had particular currency during the era of ballyhoo and the Coolidge stock-market boom. We find variations of the theme running through the editorial comment of the city newspapers and in statements given out by prominent industrialists, such as Henry Ford. It is only fair to say that it has caught the fancy of numerous writers on the farm question. For instance, Robert S. Brookings, of the Brookings Institute, wrote in 1928 to the effect that

"My own opinion is that the best means of hastening the present slow and harrowing process of agricultural regeneration is by the formation of agricultural corporations which will accomplish in organization and management what big business has accomplished for industry. Following the method pursued in the organization of the United States Steel Corporation, the most inefficient farms, which as now operated are worth less than nothing, would be paid for in safe bonds of the 'Agricultural Corporation' with some regard for their *potential value;* and the most efficient farms would receive their full present value in the same bonds, and their efficient managers become the department managers of the corporation." [7]

Somewhat along the same lines is the following quotation from *Too Many Farmers,* by Wheeler McMillen, published in 1929, with a foreword by Secretary Jardine:

"I see in the agricultural picture of the future no idea or instrumentality that lends more of high promise than the corporation farm. The basic advantage is in the economy of production costs. With this economy, with massed buying and massed selling, greater profits can be made. Profits in an industry are the basis of prosperity for those engaged in it, whether supplying capital, management or labor. The corporation farm therefore offers hope for a higher standard of living for the people in farming. A higher standard of living means a higher standard of rural civilization, better homes and better citizenship. Large scale organization, requiring high grades of services, will afford hitherto unknown opportunities in farming itself for the advancement and enrichment of capable and competent men." [8]

3. Communists and socialists carry the last suggestion a step further when they say agriculture in the United States should be collectivized as it has been in Russia. Those of this persuasion point to the superiority of the Russian collectives over the old, inefficient peasant farming methods. *Ergo,* say these, let the distressed American farmer become a collectivist.

Collective agriculture, like corporation farming, appeals particularly to those who have never followed a

[7] Brookings, *Agricultural Corporations,* pp. 7–8. Judd & Detweiler Press (1928).

[8] Reprinted from McMillen, *Too Many Farmers,* pp. 323–324, by permission of the publishers, William Morrow & Company, Inc., copyright 1929.

plow. Before passing judgment on either, perhaps it will be well to await further results. Facts, bare realities, have an uncomfortable way of upsetting the nicest of theories. All the might of the Soviet government has not succeeded in taking from the unfortunate kulaks their attachment to acres which they can call their own, or in making the huge Russian state-farms superior to forms of agricultural organization found in so-called capitalistic countries. On the western plains of the United States the corporation wheat-farmers have run into difficulty during the depression. The individual growers who have tried to imitate their example by going heavily into debt for land and expensive power-machinery are faring even worse. One curious lesson of the depression is that the small submarginal producer, whose end has been predicted from time to time from Moscow and Washington, in many cases appears to be standing up better than those who have gone in for power-farming.

Enthusiasts for collective or corporate farming too often fail to give weight to the inherent reasons why agriculture is not readily adaptable to factory or mass-production methods. Some of the things they overlook are pointed out by Alvin Johnson in his article in *The Yale Review,* for Autumn, 1932:

"Only one who has studied behind the plough can have any conception of the variety of soils in a field that looks as uniform to the city-bred economists as the green baize on a billiard table. Only one who has handled a herd of dairy cows can realize how widely they differ in character and temperament, and how much individual attention they require. The urban assumption that they are large animated animal crackers does not hold. Good agriculture requires very close-textured observation and management, not compatible with very large-scale operations. Of course one must except the business of ripping the virgin fertility out of the soil in the semi-arid wheat belts of the United States and Russia, and the production of beef and hides and wool on the vast areas of unsettled lands. Such operations may be successfully industrialized, but they will not permanently supply any nation." [9]

4. Those who see the small individual farmer as an anachronistic survival in the onward march of the industrial revolution, or who believe that agriculture's only way out of present difficulties is through a drastic reorganization such as that which has occurred over the last forty years throughout most other major industries, may usually be found in a growing group who desire to see a reduction in the number of farmers. According to them, what is needed is for a lot of farmers to go out of business.

Wall Street economists, university professors and others who have subjected the matter to office analysis, tell us that the salvation of the situation is the removal of the submarginal farmers from their farms to other lines of industry in the cities. From his book, *The Surplus Farmer,* we infer that the author, Dr. Bernhard Ostrolenk, would put the figure of those who should thus be removed at over one million.[10] This figure should be compared with the existing estimate of six and a half million farmers.

Similarly, Walter B. Pitkin, Professor of Journalism at Columbia, advocates the removal to the cities of ten million out of the twenty-seven million of population now living on farms.

[9] Johnson, "Relief from Farm Relief," reprinted from *The Yale Review,* Autumn 1932, pp. 58–59, by permission of the Editors. For evidence that state-farming in Russia is nearing collapse see two very interesting articles by Hans Zörner, *Agriculture in Russia,* in *The New Republic* of July 19 and July 26, 1933.

[10] Ostrolenk, *The Surplus Farmer,* p. XVII. Harper & Bros. (1932).

Professor Pitkin, whose judgment appears to be swayed by his association with Hickman Price's corporate wheat-ranch venture in western Texas (since failed), goes so far as to assert that those who disagree with him are conspirators against the march of progress.[11]

What gentlemen of this way of thinking fail to satisfactorily explain is what the farmers and farm families are to do in the cities. By looking too intently at one facet only of the problem, it is possible to ignore the human question whether the submarginal farmers may not be happier continuing to eke out an existence on their submarginal farms than they would be if they joined the city breadlines.

5. Another group, including official Washington, sees the solution of the problem of the agricultural surplus in the voluntary reduction of acreage under cultivation, rather than in a reduction of the number of farmers. What is needed, say these, is for the individual farmers to plant less.

The appeal of the Federal Farm Board to the farmers to do this for their own account was singularly ineffective. Even when made by those who have the interests of the farmers sincerely at heart, the argument antagonizes the individual farmer, who feels no incentive to curtail his production unless he can be assured that his neighbor will do likewise. During the depression the compulsion has been just the other way. In an endeavor to pay his debts and meet his taxes, he has had to plant more.

6. The summer and fall of 1932 saw a movement on the part of the farmers in the corn belt to take the

[11] Pitkin, "The Great Dirt Conspiracy," *The Forum Magazine*, Aug., 1931, p. 120.

situation into their own hands by creating an artificial scarcity.

The so-called farmers' strike accomplished little except to dramatize the farmers' plight for those who read the city newspapers.

Such a movement can afford only slight and temporary relief. The aim of the strikers is to raise prices by restricting the transportation of commodities from the farms to the neighboring city markets. The obstacles to their success are the over-abundant supply on the farms and the inability of the strikers to bring effective compulsion to bear against the farmers outside the movement.

Most voluntary farmers' movements, whether expressed in formal agreements or not, have to contend with similar odds.

Cut-outs of a crop, voluntary pooling arrangements (unless accompanied by a monopoly of the production), and the like, display similar weaknesses.

Contrasted with these various ways of meeting the situation are those which call for political action to be made effective. Though politicians may strive to obscure or deny the connection, every scheme to remove the existing inequality between agricultural and industrial prices in the United States, except currency inflation, revolves around our existing tariff, debt or foreign policies.

This is true of the equalization-fee and export-debenture plans, as seen in the last chapter. It is also true of the various plans for surplus-control through reduction of production, the cotton-option, land-rental, and domestic-allotment proposals, which will be explained later.

One criticism that can be made of all of these measures, involving political action, as well as of most suggestions, such as we have mentioned, to meet the agricultural crisis without political action, is that they either ignore, or meet unsatisfactorily, the dilemma facing the farmers as well as the country at large.

Since the close of the War, America has been at a crossroads in her history. Due to the change in her debtor-creditor relationship with the rest of the world, she must either allow the entry of finished goods from abroad, in payment of the accruals on the money owed her, and in payment of exports, or else restrict her production largely to a domestic basis. During the boom period the inconsistency of our anachronistic tariff, debt and foreign policies with the responsibilities of a creditor nation were camouflaged by foreign loans, which only made the matter worse in the end, and by easy money or inflationary policies followed by the Federal Reserve Banks, both of which were made possible in part by the gold importations in the years 1921–1924. Scarcely anyone appreciated the extent of the inflationary conditions which prevailed up to 1929, or the extent to which the prosperity of America's mass-production industries was due to the borrowing of foreigners and instalment buying at home.

Although before 1930 only ten per cent of our total production went into international trade, the percentage of some of our most important farm products and in some industries was much larger. In the field of raw commodities and minerals alone, the United States, although it comprises only 5.7 per cent of the world's total land surface produced in 1924—

38 per cent of the world's coal
70 " " " " " petroleum
54 " " " " " copper
40 " " " " " lead
33 " " " " " iron ore
75 " " " " " corn (maize)
25 " " " " " wheat
30 " " " " " cereals (other than wheat)
55 " " " " " cotton
53 " " " " " timber
33 " " " " " tobacco [12]

In 1929 the United States exported 55 per cent of the cotton it grew, 41 per cent of the tobacco, 36 per cent of the copper, 35 per cent of the kerosene, 33 per cent of the lard, 31 per cent of the lubricating oils, 40 per cent of the typewriters, 29 per cent of the printing machinery, 28 per cent of the sewing machinery, 23 per cent of the agricultural machinery, 21 per cent of the locomotives and 14 per cent of the automobiles.[13]

Either the United States must adjust itself to the changed situation that has existed since the War and adopt policies suited to her position as a great creditor nation in a group of interdependent nations, or else production must be restricted all along the line to the consumptive capacity of the domestic market. If the latter alternative is followed a socialistic type of state-control over production and prices appears eventually inescapable. The movement in that direction has already gone far. It is the by-product of economic nationalism both here and abroad.

Those who demand still higher tariffs and the repeal of

[12] Figures from Siegfried, *America Comes of Age*, p. 190. Harcourt, Brace & Company (1927).

[13] Figures from Moulton and Pasvolsky, *The War Debts and World Prosperity*, p. 409. The Brookings Institution (1932).

the anti-trust laws are really the prime movers in a political and economic revolution.

The reader should not imply that there is not much which can be said in behalf of a closed economic system. The United States is more nearly self-sufficient than any other of the more advanced countries. The industrial structure of the country for nearly seventy years has been built up largely behind a high tariff system. There is no question that a high tariff, to a certain extent, insulates protected industry from shocks from abroad, or that the lowering of duties too suddenly would cause many severe readjustments.

Dean Donham, of the Harvard Business School, impressed by the gloominess of the international trade outlook, has presented this point of view skillfully in his book, *Business Adrift.*

The book can quite properly be attacked because it soft-pedals the catastrophic changes which self-sufficiency necessitates for such industries as American agriculture. The book presents a point of view that appeals more strongly to the factory than to the farm, as may be judged by the author's admissions, including the following:

> "In connection with cotton we should realize that the present situation and our developing policies will tend to stimulate competing cotton growing areas. We may soon find ourselves faced with the necessity of limiting our growing of cotton mainly to the needs of our home market. This would compel readjustments in the South." [14]

In his later book, *Business Looks at the Unforeseen,* Dean Donham abandons his earlier stand, which would

[14] Donham, *Business Adrift,* p. 94. Whittlesey House (1931).

seem to have been that there was no remedy for the farm problem except for the farmers to limit production to domestic needs, by recognizing that this is "perhaps an impossible task." [15] In this second book he endorses the domestic-allotment plan, of which he has since become an outstanding advocate. Like most highly intelligent people, he is not afraid to modify his stand when it is based on inadequate evaluation of all the variables in the situation, but we wonder if his latest position should be taken to be a final judgment?

In terms of agriculture, self-sufficiency means cutting our production of cotton by more than one-half, of wheat by nearly one-quarter, of tobacco by more, and of other farm staples in greater or less degree.

For this reason, the interests of agriculture would seem to require that the United States adjust her policies to her changed debtor-creditor relationship which in turn means a reversal of our tariff, debt and foreign policies. The destruction of foreign demand for our farm and other export products is in part a direct reflection of our failure so to do.

Although there is a higher level of economic intelligence among the people generally than ever before, America has been so under the spell of so-called economic services which attempt to forecast the future by measuring the rhythm of past cycles of business activity, that we have overlooked matters which the elementary student in economics learns to accept as fundamental.

One reason why informed economic opinion has failed

[15] Donham, *Business Looks at the Unforeseen,* p. 153. Whittlesey House (1932).

to command general attention is that the economists have been too much interested in discussing among themselves their very real differences about 10 per cent of the so-called science, instead of agreeing upon the 90 per cent of their ideas about which there is less dispute.

However divergent may be their views in other fields, economists are generally agreed that in the field of international trade, within which the policy of *laissez faire* was first announced and subsequently developed, it is in the best interests of all the nations that governments interfere as little as possible with the international flow of labor, goods and capital.

In support of this statement might be instanced the appeal to Congress and President Hoover in 1930 of over one thousand teachers and professors not to revise tariff rates upward; the warning of several hundred distinguished experts at Geneva in 1927 that international barriers to trade should be lowered by their respective governments; and the manifesto, signed by forty-two Columbia professors in the year 1926, that a sweeping settlement of Reparations and War Debts was necessary.

While the author does not presume to be an economist, and there are perhaps many things in this book to which trained economists will take exception, he will, in spite of the triteness of old arguments, mention a few of the reasons why the trend of conservative economic opinion continues to adhere to the international trade viewpoint as opposed to the *ignis fatuus* of economic self-sufficiency.

The author's aim is not to write a book on agricultural economics, but to present the farm problem from a sympathetic point of view that may not be entirely free from the subconscious prejudices that inhere from his early environment in a farm community.

The Tariff. The peculiar vice of a high tariff policy at the present time is that our status as a great creditor nation calls for progressive reductions and an advanced low-tariff policy.

The most significant fact in the modern world is the economic interdependence of nations. The United States is the greatest object lesson in that world of the advantages of free trade and the fallacies of protection. Were it not for the provision written into the United States Constitution which prevents the restraint of interstate commerce, and makes possible the consequent free interstate movement of labor, goods, and capital, our mass-production industries could not have developed, as they have, so that they excel those of any other nation.

The opposition to a change in our high-tariff policy is largely based not upon principle but upon selfish advantage. Under the present laws, industry gets and enjoys, not high tariff all around, but high tariff on competing finished goods and free trade in non-competing raw materials and tropical products which enter into domestic manufacture. The resistance to a change in this policy is entrenched and stubborn. One of the subtle methods employed to sway educated opinion is the free destribution in the mail of literature in favor of extreme economic nationalism. An instance of this practice has come within the author's personal experience. For some reason, unknown to himself, he happens to be on the mailing list of the Chemical Foundation, an organization that speaks for an industry which has grown rich out of high tariff since the War. From this institution he has received in the recent past complimentary copies of a brochure by Dean Donham reprinted from the Harvard Business Review, and of Garet Garrett's *A Bubble that Broke the World* and of Samuel Crowther's, *America Self-Contained.* How many hundreds, or perhaps thousands, of copies of these works have been broadcast through the mails by this well-endowed institution the author has no means of telling. We do not mean to imply that the books in question are subsidized since they are from the pens of proficient authors who enjoy a wide audience. It is interesting that, embodying as they do, appeals to nationalistic prejudices, they apparently should be distributed gratis in behalf of an industry that, more than almost any other, owes its existence to post-War protectionism.

It is perfectly true that, even under the Hawley-Smoot Act, two-thirds of all imports are non-competitive products which are admitted into the United States duty-free. This does not mean that the law does not represent a very high level of protectionism. Before the passage of the Act a committee of the League of Nations decided, after careful investigation, that the American tariff was the highest of any nation except Spain.

The important thing is not the proportion of duty-free imports to all imports, but the volume of prospective imports of articles which are excluded altogether. It is apparent to anyone who gives the matter a second thought, that a comparison of duty-free imports with total imports tells absolutely nothing if the duties on dutiable imports are so high as to exclude the latter from the domestic market.

Our loss in trade with the rest of the world since the passage of the Hawley-Smoot Act appears from the figures of the Department of Commerce which show that, in spite of the reputed advantages enjoyed by foreign producers because of the depreciation of currencies abroad, our imports declined in dollar volume by about one-third in 1931, while in 1932 they were 37 per cent less than in 1931. The circumstance that exports declined in about the same proportion is illustrative of the fact that buying and selling are both parts of the same operation. In the long run, a nation cannot sell more than it buys, or *vice versa.*

There is an intimate relationship between protectionism and the gold problem.

With gold used chiefly as a medium of effecting international payments, it is theoretically true that, as long as a country maintains its currency from depreciation with relation to gold, the inflow of gold tends to offset the effect of a high tariff. This is because, as gold flows in and foreign currencies weaken, the price differential widens, and more efficient producers abroad can pay the tariff and still compete with domestic producers. For this reason even an exclusionist tariff will not remain exclusionist over a long period. Imports tend to creep in over the tariff walls.

Thus a new equilibrium is reached, but on a lower level of both imports and exports.

What happens can be easily grasped by taking a mathematical illustration from Alvin Harvey Hansen's, *Economic Stabilization in an Unbalanced World:*

"Suppose we start with an even balance of $4,000,000,000 of exports and $4,000,000,000 of imports. Assume now that the tariff is raised so high that all imports are checked. We now have 0 imports and $4,000,000,000 exports. Gold flows in, and prices rise in the United States relative to the rest of the world. As gold flows out of the European countries, credit is contracted and prices tend to fall. As prices fall in Europe costs of production also fall. Eventually the European costs on many articles become low enough, and the prices in America become high enough, so that the cost plus the tariff does not exceed the price. Thus as the price differential develops, more and more goods climb in over the tariff. As soon as the price differential equals the tariff, goods can flow in over the tariff wall. On the other hand, as the price differential develops costs rise in America, while prices fall in Europe. The result is that more and more American export goods are withdrawn from international markets. American exports are in the same manner curtailed. Eventually a new equilibrium is reached, at say, $2,000,000,000 of imports and $2,000,000,000 of exports." [16]

A spectacular consequence of the widening of price differentials in the United States and in foreign countries is the flight of American factories abroad. American factories can migrate to foreign countries to get on a low-cost basis, but our farms can't.

The War Debts. It is generally realized by all who have studied the situation that the international trade and monetary crisis is due, in part, to the endeavor of the creditor nations to collect unenforceable intergovernmental obligations resulting from the World War.

In regard to the War Debts, the United States is faced not with a theory, but with a situation in which a realistic treatment is imperative.

The usual arguments made in favor of requiring payment of the Debts in full are unassailable upon moral and legalistic grounds, but an insistence upon them at the present time only makes the political problem more complicated.

[16] Hansen, *op. cit.*, note 3, pp. 85–86.

From the start those economically minded have recognized that the controlling factor in the whole matter is the transfer problem. This was acknowledged as long ago as 1921 by the shrewd French statesman, Aristide Briand. Referring to reparations he then declared: "We must not lose sight of the fact that in order to pay us Germany must every year create wealth abroad for herself by developing her exports and reducing her imports to strictly necessary things. She can only do that to the detriment of the commerce and industry of the Allies. That is a strange regrettable consequence of facts."

In other words, the question from the start has been not the capacity of the debtor governments to pay, but their capacity to make payment. Payment can only be accomplished if the debtor nation can manipulate an excess of exports over imports—including in exports invisible items like shipping services, tourists expenditures and the like, as well as gold and physical goods. To effect an excess of exports over imports where there was none before, or to increase an existing excess surplus, it is necessary for the nation that does so, either to sell more abroad in one of the ways indicated, or to buy less abroad, or both.

In the final analysis, the capacity of a debtor nation to make payment abroad is the willingness of the creditor to receive. The matter does not depend upon how much the debtor can raise by taxation and spend within the country. For this reason, to link payment of the War Debts with disarmament, as President Hoover did in one of his 1932 campaign addresses, when he said: "I am hopeful of such drastic reductions of the world armaments as will save the taxpayers of the debtor countries a large part of the cost of their payments to us," obscures the real difficulty.

Although world disarmament is greatly to be desired, there is, as *The New Republic* remarked in commenting upon this utterance, "no conceivable relation between what a nation spends for its army within its own borders and its capacity to pay us back in dollars." [17]

Were we to grade our foreign debtors according to their capacity to pay, France would undoubtedly be put at the head of the list. What so many American politicians and so many millions of American citizens fail to realize is that even if France should do away with her army altogether, her capacity to make *payment* by the transfer of funds abroad would not thereby be appreciably improved.

The collapse of reparations abroad has made the statesmen and the creditor nations of Europe recognize these truths. American public men have been slow to take a realistic view, although under the Young Plan, War Debts are fiscally tied to reparations, and scarcely any sensible person today expects the War Debts to be paid in full. Because of the decline in prices since 1929 alone, the burden of the latter obligations on the debtor nations has increased by as much as 50 per cent.

The pressure upon the European debtor nations to meet intergovernmental obligations not only, on the one hand, forced them to stimulate exports and restrict imports, but also, on the other hand, was a reason impelling the creditor nations to create trade restrictions, such as tariffs and license quotas, in order to protect their own nationals from the excess of goods which the debtor nations had to dump on the world markets to obtain an

[17] *The New Republic,* August 24, 1932.

export balance. In the case of Germany, payment of reparations from 1925 onwards was made possible only by loans which private interests in the United States were willing to advance, a process which only made matters worse in the end, for it created, in addition to the War Debts, a great mass of debts due to private creditors in the United States.

Payment on the War Debts could be continued were we willing to receive goods freely, instead of barring them out by our tariff policy, were we willing to receive services, instead of preferring to subsidize our merchant marine, were we able to send enough tourists abroad, were immigrants able to make enough remittances to their relatives in the Old World, and were there enough gold in foreign central banks to bridge the gap in international payments without international monetary disturbance.

Without a fulfillment of these conditions, or at least some of them, a vote to insist upon the collection of the War Debts is a vote for economic isolation. The central key in the international deadlock is not the War Debts, but the tariff. Tariff increases, coupled with insistence upon payment by our debtors, risks the permanent loss not only of our foreign markets but of our foreign investments as well.

According to Moulton and Pasvolsky, authors of perhaps the most authoritative recent pronouncement on the subject, it will be necessary for the United States to modify its tariff and other commercial policies "even with the War Debts out of the picture," if interest on private investments abroad is to be collected.[18]

All countries have felt the force of the economic bliz-

[18] Moulton and Pasvolsky, *op. cit.*, note 13, pp. 414–415.

zard that has swept the world. With international trade strangled by rising tariffs, license quotas and foreign exchange restrictions the creditor nations have come off worse than their debtors. Thus while in 1930–1931 the foreign trade of the United States was falling 53.2 per cent, that of Great Britain fell only 36.2 per cent, and that of Germany only 39.9 per cent.

The impasse created by the War Debts is of vital concern to the American farmers.

For years, industrial Europe, and particularly Great Britain and Germany, have been the best customers we have had for American farm products.

With the world situation what it is, perhaps the greatest value to us of these uncollectible claims is that, under intelligent and resourceful leadership, it may still not be too late to use them as clubs with which to negotiate for the lowering of armaments and the opening of export markets.

Foreign Policy. A constructive attitude on the tariff and the War Debts requires a constructive foreign policy and a recognition that the only sure way to lessen the chances of war is by a restoration of economic sanity in which America, by virtue of her dominant investment position, must lead the way.

In the long run, war, with the inflation and deflation which inevitably follow war, is completely destructive of the farmers' interests. For this reason the American farmer has a vital interest in making war less likely and in removing, as far as may be possible, from the world arena the causes of war.

In view of the differences of opinion that exist as to the success and effectiveness of preventive mechanisms, such as the League of Nations, the World Court and the

Kellogg Pact, we shall not venture upon this controversial ground, but shall confine the reader's attention for a few moments to a neglected phase of the matter.

Most wars, in the last analysis, are the outcome of economic conflicts which arise between competitive national groups. In the modern world there is no weapon which is more disturbing in the field of international relations than the power of governments to deflect the course of trade. In a recent study of the economic causes of war, this conclusion is reached by Sir Arthur Salter who is impressed with dangers from the arbitrary framing, imposition and changing of tariffs.[19]

Nationalistic restrictions on world trade constitute at present a major source of international irritations. While restrictions on trade have seldom in the past lead to war, we have no assurance that the smoldering resentments created thereby may not break out into war at any time.

It is quite possible that President Wilson's greatest mistake was that he sought to establish forms and mechanisms for the settlement of international controversies instead of meeting realistically the problem of eliminating from the peace settlements the indefensible economic provisions that have ever since been a threat to the peace of the world. He staked all upon our adherence to the League Covenant and its future effectiveness. For those economically minded it is unnecessary to mention the impossible indemnity clauses, the most obvious of the frustrations of Versailles.

It is wholly outside of the sphere of this book to review the matter further here.

It is pertinent to emphasize the essential stake of

[19] Salter, *et al*, *Report on the Causes of War*, pp. 10–14. The Macmillan Company (1932).

American agriculture in the preservation of world peace and to suggest that perhaps the best way in which the course of international peace can be promoted at the present time is by efforts aimed to lessen irritations based upon conflicting economic interests. Neither the United States, nor the farmers of the United States, can have any assurance of a return of prosperity of the kind to which the American people have been accustomed in the past, without the adoption of a constructive foreign policy by our government.

America needs to promote, to the extent of her ability, the cause of world recovery because it is good business for her to do so. Only by the removal of some of the economic obstacles that at present impede the revival of international demand for our farm and other export products, can our export industries be extricated from their existing plight.

Exaggerated economic nationalism is essentially a manifestation of the failure of statesmen both here and abroad to accept realistically the outstanding economic fact of the modern world, that no nation can hope permanently to prosper without regard for the fortunes of her neighbors.

The United States itself furnishes perhaps the most perfect object lesson of how the chances of war can be lessened by the removal of trade restrictions. Mr. Norman Angell in the London journal *Foreign Affairs,* thinks Europe may profitably learn a lesson therefrom. Though economic *competition* exists between the various sections of the United States, it does not lead to open economic warfare and hence is not as dangerous as the economic *conflicts* which arise from the efforts of governments to impede the natural course of trade between differing geographical regions.

Since Mr. Angell succeeds in making clear in a few convincing paragraphs the fallacies and confusions that underlie most popular thinking on the subject of tariffs, we can appropriately close this chapter with a quotation of the same:

"Of recent years in the United States the textile industry of New England has been unable to compete with the cheaper labor and the cheaper water power of the Carolinas and other Southern States. The cotton industry has largely 'gone South.' The operatives have not followed, because in many of the Southern mills the labor is entirely negro, while in Northern mills it has been entirely white.

"Massachusetts does not demand a tariff as protection against the Southern States, still less think of war with them in this connection, because Americans have never been in the habit of thinking of the states as separate economic units and as 'foreign' to each other. No American thinks of the 'Ohio trade' as being in competition with 'Illinois trade,' as we in Europe think of 'German trade' as being in competition with 'British trade.'

"But if the American States are not to be regarded as economic units or entities why do we in Europe persist in regarding our states as such competing entities? The American is quite prepared to see the textile trade of New England ousted by the cheap negro labor of South Carolina. But if Massachusetts has to meet the competition of well-paid, white American labor in Canada, tariffs, subsidies and every other form of protection are demanded. The white American in Canada—of the same race, the same standard of life and civilization—happens to belong to a separate political sovereignty; he is therefore a 'competitor.' The poorly paid negro of the South happens to belong to the same political sovereignty. He is not therefore a 'competitor.'

"Protection arises from our conception of political nationalism. If we had not this habit in Europe of thinking in terms of distinct independent political nationalities the sense of economic competition which hag-rides us would not exist. . . .

"The great evil of protectionism is that it creates a sense of conflict of interest where fundamentally there is no conflict; it makes us fear not scarcity but plenty; makes the fruitfulness of the earth an economic disaster; makes us hate our neighbors not because they desire to take the fruits of our soil but because they desire to make the fruits of their toil available to us. It creates an inversion of reality, an Alice in Wonderland topsy-turvydom in economics."

Here it would seem we have the matter stated in terms that should appeal to our own mid-western farmers.

CHAPTER VI

HARD REALITIES

In the palmy days of 1928–1929, the prophets of the Coolidge-Hoover stock-market boom proclaimed that we were in a New Economic Era in which most of the previously accepted canons of economics, as taught in the schools, had been outmoded.

During the past three years there has come not only a realization that many of our troubles are due to misguided and uneconomic governmental policies both here and abroad, but also to a new crop of soothsayers who have despaired of the ability of men to repair the wreckage of the world's economic structure so that it could be made to function along the lines of international cooperation, as it did before the War.

Whether it can or not is beyond the power of the wisest to foretell. The hard realities of the situation are sufficiently appalling to create disquieting doubts. A frank recognition of these difficulties is necessary before we can determine the chances of a favorable outcome. We shall examine some of these hard realities in the present chapter.

The casual citizen may well inquire why, if the economists are in substantial agreement that our tariff, debt and foreign policies are in part responsible for the near breakdown of our institutions and civilization, we, instead of correcting them, have so long been headed obstinately along the wrong course.

The reasons arise from a combination of business and political factors.

The first hard reality is that over most of the last half-century dominant business circles have been out of accord with the views of the academic economists. The United States has seemed to prosper by disregarding the latter. Industry has been uncertain "of the way economics might affect its interests; it has blown hot and cold, invoking at times the inevitable laws of political economy in behalf of its own contentions, and then denouncing the professional economists for their ignorance of those laws (as business men understood them)."[1]

Differences of attitude have resulted in mutual distrust. The claim of economists to public confidence is based upon their position as impartial seekers after truth. To the extent of their pretensions as such, they are disqualified from taking sides in behalf of conflicting economic interests.

This unfitness, while it limits the effectiveness of their voice in the direction of national policy, makes them especially useful servants of the general public. A particular economic interest may profit from the adoption of policies that are economically unsound, but the public, in the long run, never does. The ultimate interest of the public is always served by the unvarnished truth.

The modern industrialist, who has had so large a hand

[1] Fetter, "The Economists and the Public," *The American Economic Review,* Vol. XV, No. 1 (March, 1925), p. 18.

in shaping the destinies of the country, is, as distinguished from the economist, ordinarily so engrossed in practical affairs that he is inclined to dismiss as "theory" the views of academic economists when they do not subserve the end of producing immediate profits for himself, his stockholders and business associates.

As anyone with a cursory knowledge of the facts of American history is aware, no nation in modern times ever did more to foster the rapid growth of industry than did the United States during the latter half of the nineteenth century. Among the princely favors might be instanced a land policy which resulted in the rapid alienation of priceless national resources, public grants to railroads and other private enterprises, the relaxation of the corporation laws of various states to suit the requirements of finance and speculation, special favors in taxation and general legislation, and a tariff system designed to effectuate the transfer, under the guise of law, of wealth from the producers and consumers in general, to the manufacturers and those dependent upon them.

During the time when governmental policy was thus directed to accentuate the growth of industry, industry did not appeal to the laws of political economy against these paternalistic largesses. As Professor Frank A. Fetter, in an address made in 1925 while president of the American Economic Association, interestingly told, the appeal of industry to the public and to Congress was "to give quickly and generously."

When the rise of great corporations in the eighties thrust to the front the general problems connected with the control of monopoly, the division of viewpoint between trained students and the average "practical" business men began to grow into a schism that has persisted through all the intervening years. Professor Fetter explains how this happened as follows:

"The public was beginning to demand some regulation of this pseudo-competition, some control of the ambiguous private industries that were performing in large measure public functions. Against all such attempts to regulate or control corporate industries, business leaders protested. The beneficiaries of special favors from the government and the public declared loudly that private business must be left untouched by government. But they did not in remorse offer to return the gifts they had received. Manufacturers saw no inconsistency in continuing to laud the high statesmanship of 'protective' tariffs, in the same breath in which they proclaimed the sanctity of the great economic principle of free competition.

"Here began to appear more clearly a paradoxical contrast between the views of trained economists and the views of business men in respect to economic questions. The exponent of practical business invoked abstract principles very dogmatically whenever he thought they favored his case; the academic economist became more realistic, recognizing the conflict of facts with the old assumptions. Rarely from economists but constantly from business and financial interests have been heard, and continue to be heard, such phrases as 'the eternal laws of political economy,' 'unchangeable economic principles,' 'the fundamental law of supply and demand.' The economists have not lost faith in the virtues of free competition in industry where it actually exists or is possible, as among the members of fairly equal economic classes. But they see clearly that in actual life these conditions have become more and more rare. Regulation and control may be necessary at times to conserve certain human values not reducible to terms of profits or of material wealth, or to restore and replace competition where it has been lost in special privilege and economic inequality. On many of the gravest economic issues of the last third of a century the academic economists have supported the popular demand as against the views in dominant business circles. So on railroad rates and public utility regulation, on immigration, on social insurance, on the general question of labor organization, on many features of the organization of the banking system, the establishment of postal savings and of the parcel post. . . .

"In consequence, the spokesmen of business lose few opportunities to disparage the academic economist, while they profess high regard for political economy as they conceive it to be. But this infallible code of wisdom only practical business men are competent to interpret." [2]

Foremost among the hard realities which retard the movement toward international coöperation is the cultural lag between the trained student, who takes a realistic view of the nation's problems, and the average business mentality, which is inclined to view matters in terms of private profits.

A second hard reality is that the economic structure of the country has been built on a basis of paternalistic support and thus a situation has been created that makes radical reform almost impossible. Even the free trader is forced to admit that the lowering of old tariffs, unless gradual, may result in unbearable hardships for many. "It is not," says Sir Arthur Salter, "just a matter of a few vested interests (as it is when new tariffs are first proposed); for a vast capital expenditure has been invested which, if the basis were removed, might be largely lost. A mass of population has become trained and specialized in certain occupations, which they cannot easily change." [3]

The difficulty of drastic correction appears when we realize that no one now living has been through the experience of changing from an insulated to a free system.

England went through such a change, over a century ago, in spite of passion and prejudice and the opposition

[2] *Ibid.*, p. 19.
[3] Salter, *Recovery*, p. 204. The Century Company (1932).

of vested economic and political interests; and England's conversion is the outstanding example in modern times of such a movement reaching a successful culmination in a great nation. When Adam Smith wrote *The Wealth of Nations,* he remarked that it was idle to expect that Great Britain would ever come to the "natural" system of free trade; yet within seventy years the impossible had happened. The actual change itself took less than ten years. It began with unexpected agitation in Manchester, which had become the center of the exporting interests.

A third hard reality is that in a democratic government, power, regardless of convenient phrases to the contrary, resides in the so-called pressure groups. The great majority of people in a democracy may know what they want, but they do not know how to get it. The pressure groups, on the other hand, are skilled in the arts of influencing public opinion and political manipulation. They are well organized and constantly alert, while the average voter's interest in how his government is run frequently does not survive a perfunctory ballot-casting at election-time. The pressure groups do not know party lines and bring pressure to bear equally upon members of both the great political parties. They work inside as well as outside of Congress. They always have. As Arthur Krock, the talented Washington correspondent of the *New York Times,* has observed: "The combination of the Greeks outside the walls and the Greeks inside the Trojan horse can take many a legislative Troy."

Foremost among the associations with central agencies at the national capital whose business it is to exert pressure upon legislative or administrative officials to obtain favors for special interests, or to see that nothing is done that may injure them, are those which represent "big business," including such organizations as follows:

American Chamber of Commerce
National Association of Manufacturers
American Manufacturers' Export Association
Institute of American Meat Packers
American Automobile Association
National Canners' Association
Council of American Cotton Manufacturers
Founders' Association
Lumber Manufacturers' Association
Manufacturing Chemists' Association of America
Highway Industries Association
Interstate Cottonseed Crushers' Association
Merchants and Manufacturers' Association
Southern Industrial Education Society
United States Sugar Manufacturers' Association
Western Petroleum Refiners' Association

Rivaling these in power are others too numerous to mention. In distinct groupings may be separated organizations which represent the public utilities, union labor, the veterans and reform organizations, among which are such well-known associations as the Anti-Saloon League, the Crusaders and the National Association of Women for the Repeal of the Eighteenth Amendment.[4]

Nor can we omit the pressure groups that represent agriculture. Because of the inarticulateness of the farmers in general, the cause of the farmers in the national

[4] See Siegfried, *America Comes of Age*, pp. 249–253. Harcourt, Brace and Company (1927).

capital is largely pleaded by the leaders of special organizations reflecting pragmatically, if imperfectly, the gravamen of the farmers' legislative complaints and demands.

A fourth hard reality is the scarcity of public men with a national point of view. For this reason, a wise and unafraid President, when he arises, can nearly always enforce his will upon a Congress that is distracted by conflicting sectional and economic interests. Compelled by his training to develop a propensity for the discovery of common denominators between the diverse ideas and purposes of many people, he can, if he is a successful executive, get his program enacted by appealing over the heads of Congress to the verdict of like-minded people throughout the nation. The average Congressman, on the other hand, constantly sacrifices an aggregate point of view to that of particular sectional or economic interests. In order to get elected or reëlected to office he must get as much as he can for the dominant or most vociferous interests in his district and, in turn, arrange that they bear the least possible share of the common burden. He is inclined to view his job as a delegated responsibility to see that nothing is put over on the district or state which he represents.

Although there are many honest, able and patriotic men in both houses of Congress, as well as some demagogues, at no time in our history has Congress fallen lower in public esteem than during the last decade.

For this, it can fairly be said that the members of Congress are not wholly to blame. Partly responsible are the vastness of the country, the diversity of its conflicting economic interests and their specialization.

We have not a homogeneous country such as England, or party responsibility such as is found in the British parliamentary system. Instead, we have a system of divided responsibility, with members of Congress elected for different terms from that of the Executive. An administration that has been rebuked at the polls must continue for the last half of its term to deal with a hostile legislature. Again where the Executive is a poor politician (using the term in the better sense of one skilled in the transaction of public affairs) there is no leadership, even with a party majority in both houses of Congress. This was illustrated in the first half of President Hoover's term when the Hawley-Smoot bill was passed in spite of a fairly general agreement of its unwisdom. Of the feeling at the time Professor F. W. Taussig, of Harvard, has told the following story:

"About a year ago, when the Tariff Act of 1930 was in the making, a friend of mine, a Swiss, a scholar and also something of a diplomat, came to visit me, and in the course of a friendly conversation spoke of a puzzle in our public affairs which he could not unravel. Having been in Washington and in New York, he had talked with people of all sorts and kinds, with members of the Cabinet and other officials in Washington, with Senators and Congressmen, with bankers and business men, with foreign diplomats, with newspaper men, with Republicans as well as with Democrats, with persons of all kinds and very different points of view. All had said to him the same things about the then pending tariff bill. Nobody thought it a good measure; nobody wished to see it enacted. It had not a friend. Nobody had any expectation that it would stem the business depression. Some Republicans remarked that they would have to proclaim in public that it would 'help business,' but in their hearts they could not think so. The President of the United States himself [so the puzzled foreigner was told] was much in doubt whether he should veto the act or let it become law.

"And yet, though everybody disliked the bill, everybody said it would infallibly be passed. Unwelcome and unsatisfactory as all declared it, all said that it would find its way upon the statute book. 'What,' my friend asked me, 'is the explanation of this extraordinary situation? How does it happen that something which nobody wants done nevertheless is something which everybody is sure will be done?' "[5]

For the grotesque Hawley-Smoot Act, it is only fair to say that the Republican party, the traditional friend of protectionists, was not wholly to blame. The Hawley-Smoot Act, as well as the ridiculous rates in the budget-balancing Act of 1932 on coal, copper, oil and lumber (of all of which we export more than we import), were made possible by the votes of Democratic senators. Due to regional specialization and the increasing specialization within industries and occupations, party lines seldom hold on controversial questions of public finance, agriculture or utility regulation. Gone are the intense party loyalties of earlier generations. Electioneers still appeal to the hypnotic names of Jefferson, on the one hand, and of Lincoln, on the other, but as a matter of fact both the great political parties are little more than loose confederations, held together by the hope of party spoils, but rent with economic and sectional cleavages. Of party principles, little remains except opposing traditions and tendencies.

Nor can we blame recent high tariffs wholly on the manufacturers. Although in 1930 it was estimated that on but two and a half per cent of agricultural produce were tariff duties fully effective, they were then partially effective on approximately 34 per cent more, ranging

[5] Taussig, "What the Tariff Has Done to Us," *The Atlantic Monthly*, November, 1931, p. 669.

anywhere from a small and doubtful amount, as on hard spring wheat, to a positive and fairly persistent degree of protection, as in the case of butter.[6] While with respect to the percentage on which duties are partially effective the benefit is often doubtful because the effect is purely local, the Republican party in more than one election has attempted to hold the farmers in line with the general plea that tariff protection has become essential to agriculture generally.

Likewise, it should not be forgotten that there are certain agricultural groups, such as the cane-sugar growers of Louisiana and the beet growers of the Rocky Mountain States, whose self-interest makes them confirmed protectionists.

Sugar is a good example of the political power which the strategy of the situation gives to a cohesive minority in the process of horse-trading that has ever been characteristic of tariff-making. The sugar duty is always used by protectionists to negative the argument that a tariff hurts the farmers as a group. The United States census figures, which include as sugar-growers all who produce molasses or maple sugar, or sorghum for cattle feed, show that only about two and a third per cent of all the farmers in the country grow sugar. The small percentage of real sugar-growers exert economic and political power far beyond their numerical strength, because they are congregated in selected regions, whose representatives get what they want by uniting with other minority groups. The minorities win by uniting at the expense of the whole country.

[6] Hibbard, "The Agricultural Tariff of 1922 and a Look Ahead," *Journal of Farm Economics,* Vol. XII, No. 1 (Jan., 1930), p. 70.

The Hawley-Smoot bill became a law by concessions made by dominant economic and political interests to various specialized agricultural groups, which were in turn minorities of the total farming population,—itself a minority of all the people in the country.

The last, no less than the total farming population, were losers.

A sixth hard reality is the persistence and strength of popular prejudices. We are still victims of a distrust of participation in world affairs, which was a mass-reaction to the horrors of the World War and the chicanery of the peace treaty. This feeling is strongest in the vast tracts of land in the interior of the United States, where the problems of international politics are unknown and where the people generally are not deeply versed in economic knowledge. Although there is no class that has more to gain from a revision of our tariff, debt and foreign policies than the farmers of the Middle West, there is less understanding of the need for a revision, at least so far as the War Debts are concerned, the farther inland one goes from the Atlantic seaboard. It is an ironic circumstance that there is a better understanding along the Atlantic seaboard, which pays the largest share of the country's income tax and on which likewise would fall the major burden of any increase in taxes which might be necessitated by a complete cessation of payments from the debtor governments.

Practical party managers are inclined to take a frank, objective view of the complications caused by these hard realities, as the Democratic platforms of 1928 and 1932, for instance, reflect. In the earlier year at Houston, the

Democrats, yielding to the siren of political expediency, adopted a tariff plank that differed little from the Republicans, thus committing an ill-advised blunder in view of the subsequent dénouement of the bankruptcy of Republican leadership in matters of tariffs, debt and foreign policy.

Though the 1932 platform declaration of the Democrats in favor of a "competitive tariff" represented a shift away from the Houston apostasy toward the historic stand of the party on the tariff, it fell far short of a complete recantation. This was admitted by the Democratic nominee who, in explaining at Sioux City the platform declaration as being for a tariff "that equalizes the difference in the cost of production" at home and abroad, frankly added:

> "I appreciate that the doctrine thus announced is not widely different from that preached by Republican statesmen and politicians."

In the 1932 campaign the Democrats denounced the excessive rates of the Hawley-Smoot Act but failed to take a sharply contrasting stand from the Republicans with respect to the endorsement of the protective principle. So far as the tariff was concerned, the issues were sharply drawn only with respect to "reciprocal arrangements with other nations," the Republicans standing firmly for a preservation of the *status quo* and the Democrats advocating the principle of offering concessions in rates to other countries in return for similar concessions on American goods.

With respect to the tariff and the War Debts, the only advanced position in the campaign was that taken by the Socialist candidate, Mr. Norman Thomas, who from the start had not the slightest chance of winning.

In spite of these undeniable realities, the cause of international coöperation, so far as the United States is concerned, is far from hopeless.

In the first place, resourceful leadership and effective party government has reappeared. Mr. Roosevelt's tariff stand during the campaign, as we have ventured to suggest it, evidences an understanding of the difficulties of the situation and a realization that time must necessarily elapse for public opinion to undergo a fundamental transition. Behind a liberal administration there is an impressive majority in both Houses of Congress of the party committed traditionally to the policy of a low-tariff and international reciprocity.

Secondly, the near collapse of our economic and governmental institutions has created a national psychology that welcomes change. Unless there is decided improvement in economic conditions generally, the demand for radical change will become more insistent. Although it is undeniable that the public sentiment of the country still is against radical changes in the tariff, a business-like settlement of the War Debts, and any extensive excursions in world economic matters, and that the existence of this public sentiment must be treated objectively as a matter of practical politics, public opinion can reverse itself within the span of a few years, and politicians even quicker, as has been shown in the case of prohibition. The movement for the repeal of the Eighteenth Amendment has shown how thoroughly and completely politicians can change their stand, after there has been a fundamental change of public opinion in the nation at large.

Public opinion is due to turn against economic nationalism in its various manifestations, unless the American people are willing to embrace without regrets the alternative of compulsory restriction of output all along the line, with its logical consequence, unpredictable extensions of the area of governmental price-control.

Third, and last, there are other groups, in the aggregate, no less important from a political standpoint than the farmers, who would prefer to have the country move in the direction of a free rather than a closed economic system.

On the matter of the tariff, War Debts and foreign policy, the old lines of conflict between the farm and the factory are no longer sharply drawn.

Some of our biggest industries benefit little, if at all, from high protection, because, without tariff protection, they excel foreign competitors in the economies of mass-production, the technique of large-scale management, and in mass-advertising and mass-distribution. They can only remain busy and profitable by selling their excess products abroad.

Another large group of industries which receive no advantage from high tariffs and which suffer when for any reason the productive capacity of the country is artificially restricted are the railroads, light, power and telephone companies, and public utilities in general.

Vitally interested in the situation, likewise, are those banking groups that are identified with foreign investment, and all the various groups that are dependent in one way or another upon international trade, the shipping interests, and exporters and importers in general.

These are economic realities which necessarily will play

a part in shaping the course of future events in the United States.

The tide may be slow in turning, but when it does turn, those farmers who stand to gain rather than lose by international coöperation—and this includes the great bulk of the farmers with the conspicuous exception of such groups as the sugar-growers, who are dependent upon protection,—may find themselves moving in a resistless current which will sweep aside obstacles and definitely and finally carry the nation from its high-tariff moorings.

Or is it true that the dikes are so strong that the tide cannot turn?

CHAPTER VII

TRANSITION

DURING the national campaign of 1932, Mr. Roosevelt divided his farm relief program into two parts, an emergency plan and a permanent program.

During the campaign, the Republican speakers, and particularly Mr. Hoover, stressed the old hokum about tariff protection for the farmer. A pledge was also made to continue governmental assistance to the coöperative marketing movement. The principal contribution of a new nature offered, other than the administration's general program for the use of government credit to restore the general economic structure, was that by Mr. Hoover for "the utilization of the war debts to advantage agriculture and labor." How this was to be accomplished was not explained by the President. Neither was it explained whether payment for our products by the foreign buyers was to be made by (1) shipments of goods, (2) their selling us goods and services, or (3) by their selling us securities.

The Democrats' stand on farm relief during the campaign was related to their stand on the tariff, to which we referred at the close of the last chapter.

In his speech at Springfield, Illinois, Mr. Roosevelt took the position that the farm question was a political problem, stating that "the Federal government owes it to agriculture to see that it gets a fair price for its products" and explaining "that much in this direction" can be done "by a properly adjusted tariff."

"Pending the relief that will be afforded by a properly adjusted tariff policy" he advocated measures "to give the farmers immediate tariff benefits." We have seen how in the 1928 campaign Governor Smith, while taking a highly protective stand, endorsed the "principle" of the equalization-fee, without specifically committing himself to any of the plans which for some six years previously had occupied the attention of Congress. Taking a leaf from the record of that campaign, Mr. Roosevelt, in his speech at Topeka, stated that it would be his purpose to compose the differences between the various plans designed to give the farmers immediate tariff benefits and, without committing himself to any particular plan by name, announced his whole-hearted accord with any plan which would meet six particular requirements.

These "specifications" in brief were:

1. The plan must provide for the producer of farm staples such as wheat, cotton, corn (in the form of hogs) and tobacco, a tariff benefit over world prices equivalent "to the benefit given by the tariff to industrial products." This result must be accomplished in a manner so as not to stimulate further production.

2. The plan must be self-financing.

3. It must not invite retaliation from European countries on the ground of dumping.

4. It must be decentralized, so far as possible, in its administration.

5. It must be constituted so that "it can be withdrawn whenever the emergency has passed and normal foreign markets have been reëstablished."

6. It must be voluntary.

From the above it will be seen that the so-called "plan" was intended as an emergency measure.

A significant feature of the permanent program was the assurance of "a properly adjusted tariff."

When Mr. Roosevelt came into power on March 4th, the situation of the country did not permit the waste of two or three years in debating what was the best thing to do.

All the banks in the nation were closed. Between 12,000,000 and 15,000,000 men were out of work.

Direct-action incidents in the corn belt indicated that thousands of farmers were on the verge of revolt against the constituted authorities.

There was an immediate necessity that the federal government, which alone could save the situation, do something quickly.

One of the first acts of the new administration was to get the farm organization leaders together into a general conference.

The price-elevation features contained in the 1933 Farm Bill, with the grant to the Secretary of Agriculture, of vast powers to deal with the emergency, are an outgrowth of the recommendations made by the special committee authorized at that conference.

These provisions, if not the whole bill, represent a series of compromises between people with different ideas.

In submitting the bill to Congress for consideration

the President accompanied it with a brief message in which he frankly said "it is a new and untrod path" but "an unprecedented condition calls for the trial of new means to rescue agriculture." He further admitted: "If a fair administrative trial of it is made and it does not produce the hoped for results, I shall be the first to acknowledge it and advise you."

We shall not discuss here the mortgage-relief and inflation provisions which were added to the bill in the course of its passage through Congress. The first of these is generally recognized to be a sound and highly salutary measure. The latter contains explosive possibilities, the outcome of which cannot be predicted. The most interesting features of the bill are the price-elevation provisions.

Since, at the time this is written, these, likewise, have not been put into general operation, we must, with the President, reserve judgment as to whether they, or any feature of them, will need to be abandoned as unworkable.

Success or failure depends largely upon the skill and devotion of those charged with the task of administration. It depends to an even greater extent upon the coöperation of the average "dirt" farmer.

Incidentally, no class, perhaps, is inclined to be more skeptical of these provisions than the unlettered "dirt" farmer who knows from practical experience that agricultural production, unlike factory production, cannot be automatically controlled by letting a part of the plant stand idle; but, on the contrary, is dependent less upon acreage than upon the unpredictable factors like rainfall and the seasons.

For the benefit of the general reader the main features of the bill, other than the mortgage-relief and inflation provisions, will be briefly described, before an attempt is made to relate them to the administration's general scheme for a controlled domestic economy, or to contrast the latter with the objectives of the President's permanent farm program, as indicated in his compaign and in some of his speeches since his election.

The bill makes the price-elevation provisions of the bill applicable to cotton, wheat, field corn, hogs, rice, tobacco, and milk and its products.

Two outstanding features of the legislation (which show its provisional character) are the large measure of discretion given to the Secretary of Agriculture to select means for carrying out the purposes of the legislation and the power of the President to terminate practically at his discretion the operation of the legislation as a whole or with respect to any commodity.

The Department of Agriculture has indicated that it will apply different features of the legislation to different commodities, fitting a single feature or a combination of features to a single crop as circumstances warrant. Thus the domestic allotment plan will be applied to wheat; the land-rental features to certain types of tobacco; and a combination of the land-rental and option schemes to cotton.

A tax on processors, which is an essential characteristic of the domestic allotment plan, plus an appropriation of one hundred million dollars, is expected to take care of administrative expenses and the payment of rental and benefit payments to growers in return for agreements to restrict production.

The price objective of the bill is to restore for each of the commodities in question approximately its pre-war (1909–1914 average) purchasing parity with the things which farmers buy. In the case of tobacco an average price for the 1919–1929 period is taken instead of the pre-war years.

The principal means by which this price objective is to be reached are the option, land-rental and domestic allotment plans.

So much has been done to familiarize the public with these schemes that only a bare explanation will be given here. Although it is likely that before this book appears, the method of application to different crops may be varied, we shall discuss only such features of the program as have been unfolded at the time this is written (July, 1933).

Each of the three plans which we have mentioned is a device to induce the growers voluntarily to restrict production, in consideration of compensatory benefits supplied by the federal government.

Option Plan. This plan was originally proposed in Congress and sponsored by the Chairman of the Senate Committee on Agriculture, Senator Smith of South Carolina, who deemed it a more practicable method of handling the cotton situation than the domestic allotment plan. It is limited to cotton. The bill authorizes the Secretary of Agriculture, with money obtained from the Reconstruction Finance Corporation, to complete the transfer of title to himself of all cotton owned by government agencies or on which government agencies have made loans. The Secretary may thereupon offer to the cotton-grower options on this cotton up to the amount by which he agrees to reduce his output. The grower may accept delivery of the optioned cotton, or the Secretary of Agriculture may sell it for his account. In no event is he liable for any losses through holding the cotton or on account of carrying charges. The successful working of the plan is dependent upon output being reduced to such an extent that it will cause a rise in the market price of cotton sufficient to enable the optioned cotton, representing the carry-over from previous crops in the hands of, or under the control of, government agencies, to be disposed of at a profit over the option figure. The Secretary must dispose of all cotton by March 1, 1936.

Under the program announced by the Department of Agriculture in June, 1933, a combination of this plan with land-rental and processing-tax features has been offered to the cotton-growers. A fund of about $125,000,000 is being raised by a tax on the cotton processors. The grower who agrees to cut his output receives a minimum rental varying according to the past yield of his land. Under one contract offered by the government he had the right to take an option at 6 cents a pound on an amount of government-owned cotton, corresponding to the voluntary reduction of his output. If the price goes up as a result of the plan, he can sell the cotton at a profit; if it goes down, he does not exercise the option, and loses nothing. If the grower was not attracted by this speculation, he had the choice under another contract to forego the option entirely, and in lieu thereof receive a somewhat higher rental on that part of his acreage which is taken out of production.

The processing tax, to pay for the rental benefits, has met with opposition from some of the textile interests and in other quarters. It has been estimated that even if the entire tax is passed on to the consumer it should not add more than 5 cents to the cost of a $1.50 shirt.

Land-Rental Plan. The bill authorizes the use of this plan in connection with any crop to which the bill is applicable. Since we have already indicated how the plan works in connection with the program as to cotton, we shall not attempt a further explanation. An important feature of the land-rental scheme is that restrictions are placed upon the use of the leased land.

Domestic-Allotment Plan. This plan appears to have originated independently with several different agricultural economists. It would seem to be the composite product of various minds. In his book, *Agricultural Reform in the United States,* Professor J. D. Black gives credit to Dr. W. J. Spillman, of the Department of Agriculture, for presentation of the central idea in preliminary form as far back as 1926. Professor Black, himself, is responsible for the elaboration of a somewhat different scheme which was published in 1929 for the first time in his volume already mentioned. Other names prominently associated with the development of this plan are those of Professor M. L. Wilson, of the University of Montana, and W. R. Ronald, publisher of the Mitchell (S. D.) *Evening Republican.*

Briefly, the basic principle of the original domestic-allotment plan was to divide the market for that part of a crop consumed within the United States from the market for the part which enters into world trade. For the first, the producer would receive the world price, plus the amount of the tariff duty on the commodity; for the remainder, the world price only.

The program which the Department of Agriculture has announced for wheat illustrates the manner in which the modified domestic allotment features of the bill will no doubt be utilized for the handling of other commodities. An effort is made to decentralize the administration of the plan as far as possible. Through state and county organizations (the county organizations being composed of the wheat-growers themselves) the farmers are offered an opportunity to sign contracts entitling them to benefit payments on that part of their wheat crop ordinarily consumed in the domestic market. The allotment for each state and each county is determined at Washington with the aid of census figures which show previous wheat acreage by states and counties. The computations thus made fix the allotments for each county. In return for the benefit payments, each grower participating in the plan agrees to reduce his wheat acreage for 1934 and 1935 to the extent that may be required by the Department of Agriculture, not in excess of a maximum of 20 per cent of the average amount of wheat planted by him over the period of the last three years. Since a claim of too much by any one farmer will rob his neighbors in the same county, it is in the interest of the other growers in the county to prevent overstatements or errors in the past production reported by any single grower.

Money to pay the special benefits is to be raised by taxing the millers and other processors. It has been estimated that if a processing tax of thirty cents a bushel is levied, a fund of from $130,000,000 to $150,000,000 in the next wheat-growing year can be collected, and the cost to the consumer of a loaf of bread should not be increased more than half a cent.

Publicity as to the relationship between the processing tax and the price paid to producers is relied upon in part to restrain profiteering and pyramiding of the tax by distributors and others. As an additional fulcrum the Secretary of Agriculture is given the drastic power to require licenses of processors, associations of producers and others handling any agricultural commodity or product, or any competing commodity or product in the current of interstate or foreign commerce, such licenses to be revocable after hearing and proof of violation by the licensee of the terms and conditions of the permit.

The license provisions are in addition to the power given to the Secretary to enter into marketing agreements with processors and distributors of any agricultural commodity or product which is in the current of interstate or foreign commerce.

If the imposition of processing tax upon any basic agricultural commodity covered by the bill results, or will result, in an excessive shift in consumption between such commodity and a competing product (such as rayon, silk, linen and oleomargarine), the Secretary is authorized to levy a tax on the processors of the competing product.

Other provisions of the bill, such as (1) a tax on floor stocks at the time the processing tax goes into effect (2) a refund of tax on products exported out of the United States and (3) an exemption of the tax upon products used for charitable purposes or processed by the producer in his own household, or in cases where the product would tend to be driven out of certain uses by the levying of the tax, while important, do not call for extended comment here.

Reduced to the simplest terms, all the three plans—the option, land-rental and domestic-allotment proposals—offer a price-bait to induce the limitation of acreage. Each, in essence, is a device to subsidize the individual grower, if he will agree to restrict output.

Unlike the equalization-fee and export-debenture plans agitated in Congress during the Harding-Coolidge and Hoover régimes, the Roosevelt farm bill is contrived so as to avoid stimulation of production with an increase in price to the producer. The purposes of the bill cannot, however, be effected as to any particular agricultural commodity covered by the bill, unless a preponderant number of growers agree to accept the benefit payments in return for agreements to cut acreage.

Unlike the equalization-fee the subsidy to the participating grower does not fall on the farmers as a class; unlike the export-debenture plan it is not financed solely out of the Federal Treasury, but is collected out of special taxes on processors. In other words, the plans are self-financing.

Because the underlying thought of the bill is to raise the prices of agricultural commodities by cutting down exportable surpluses, which under present world conditions go into the domestic carry-over, it is, over the long-term, inconsistent with the idea that the way to reduce the carry-over is to open up foreign markets by the removal of barriers upon international trade.

This conflict appears most clearly in the provision contained in the bill for compensatory tariff-increases (designated in the bill as compensating taxes) upon competing foreign products, which otherwise might undersell domestic products upon which a processing tax has been levied.

Perhaps the greatest drawback to the bill is the complexity of its provisions and the difficulty of their administration over a country of continental proportions.

The following editorial comment in *The New Republic* of September 21, 1932, upon the domestic-allotment plan, expresses a point of view that can possibly be expressed as to the entire price-elevation scheme of the bill:

> "In itself, the domestic-allotment plan of course looks like just another mustard plaster for the aches and pains of a hopelessly sick capitalist system. It might in fact turn out to be just that. . . . It does have importance, however, as the most reasonable of all the schemes to deal with the agricultural emergency which do not contemplate revolution in the ownership of property. Those who, on the other hand, do not want collapse into primitive and inefficient farming and, on the other, do not desire or do not expect revolutionary change, are under an obligation either to accept this plan or suggest a better one."

In the past the economic life of the nation has been largely an unconscious thing, in the sense that no human mind or group of minds has seen the whole picture, and certainly no human mind or group of minds has directed the functioning of the complex organism. Human steering there has been, but it has been the steering of men and organizations seeking their own particular gain, seeing their own particular sources of supply and their own particular markets, but without seeing at all clearly the functioning of the process as a whole.

Through the interplay of forces, largely impersonal, a sort of automatic balance has tended to be maintained, and the nation as a whole has prospered and become rich and powerful, in spite of the danger, which has always existed, that the balance would be permanently upset by the over-reaching of weak groups by the more powerful, or that the self-acting agents, which after every crisis in our economic life have operated to bring about a new equilibrium, might fail to bring recovery in time to save our institutions from disaster.

The latter danger was never before so real as it was on March 4, 1933. No popular government, resting upon the consent of the governed, can long survive a condition such as then existed.

The 1933 Farm Bill, to which the National Industrial Recovery Act is a companion measure, is a step to substitute for the automatic forces which have brought recovery from past depressions a central intelligence where there has been none before.

The pattern of each rests not upon force, but upon persuasion and coöperation.

As may be expected from the vast scope of the experiment, both bills are tentative and undoubtedly contain provisions which will prove to be unworkable either in whole or in part. Secretary Wallace has himself admitted; "in some ways, perhaps, it [the Farm Bill] is as crude as the first automobile."

We shall not therefore venture to discuss possible legal or other technical difficulties, but instead shall confine ourselves to certain fundamental criticisms, which even sympathetic critics are forced to recognize.

In passing, we may safely hazard the assertion that, of the two laws, the National Industrial Recovery Act is probably the more workable, because industry is more susceptible of central control than agriculture, as the latter is at present organized.

As to the fundamental criticisms we shall be brief. These are applicable to economic planning as a general theory.

1. Under the pressure of war-time necessity vast powers to control the industrial activities of the nation were entrusted to the federal government. But then the objective was single and clear. We had a plan then but the plan was directed at winning the War. The almost insuperable obstacle to economic planning on a wide scale is the difficulty of finding human brains capable of planning wisely and well.

It is questionable wisest and best-trained minds, given the power, possess sufficient knowledge to comprehend all the variable influences, any one of which, if disregarded, may bring disaster to the paper design.

2. A government that takes upon itself the task of representing the conflicting interests of capital, labor and the consumer is apt to get into an impossible situation. Any scheme for the subjection of our economic life to conscious centralized control has to be administered by political agencies, with all the drawbacks which control in such hands implies. There is the danger that the interests of the more or less inarticulate groups may be sacrificed to political expediency. There is the increased danger of governmental corruption. Even greater, from the standpoint of the farmers, is the danger that the machinery of governmental control may fall in the hands of interests unsympathetic to their economic ambitions.

It was Bacon who expressed the great truth, "Prosperity breedeth vice, while adversity discovereth virtue."

Throughout all history, reform movements, originating in times of social strain, have faltered and gone down under the weight of public indifference when once men's minds again became engrossed in the pursuit of private gain.

We shall do well to recall that the exaltation of public spirit, which came during the War and which furnished a sounding-board for Wilsonian idealism, was succeeded by the shamelessness of Harding normalcy. So, too, there is a real danger that the elaborate system of controls provided for in the New Deal may, with a change of administration, be employed by big business and organized labor as instruments for the plunder of the middle classes under the guise of law.

3. A third fundamental criticism of the Farm Bill and the National Industrial Recovery Act is their apparent inconsistency, over the long term, with what Mr. Roosevelt on various occasions has indicated would be the permanent objectives of his farm program.

Called into power at a time when the country at large had little hope that the government could do anything really effective to subdue the forces of internal disintegration, it is fair to say that the response of Mr. Roosevelt and his advisers to the situation has been practical and realistic rather than inherently congruous.

The most important issue before the American people is whether we are going to produce for world trade or go on a domestic basis.

The Farm Bill, with its provision for compensating tariff-increases, and the National Industrial Recovery Act, which empowers the President even to embargo competing foreign products, are steps definitely in the direction of a self-contained economy. A definite aim of each is to cut down production more nearly to domestic consumptive capacity.

On the other hand, Mr. Roosevelt and various members of his cabinet, particularly Secretaries Hull, Roper and Wallace, have frequently emphasized the importance of international trade and the need for reducing the barriers and impediments to world commerce.

Perhaps the best characterization of the present period is that it is a period of transition. The administration does not pretend to have a formula to cure the country's ills. It questions even whether, in a situation which is subject to rapid changes, any formula can be found.

Like the President, his circle of advisers, though recruited in part from university classrooms, are intensely realistic. They are not likely to repeat the mistake of President Wilson, in underestimating the political factors in the situation.

They know that in nearly every country there are powerful vested interests which are seeking the retention and even the increase of protective duties on special articles. They know that, in all countries affected, the War Debts continue delicate political issues; and that the prospective value of these claims, as a club to enforce trade concessions abroad, has been jeopardized by long delay and the ineptitude of post-War statesmanship.

They are not unaware of the hard realities of domestic politics and of the part played therein by tradition, conservatism, ignorance and demagoguery.

Though aware of the importance of international trade, they appreciate that, in the present state of the world, the reduction of barriers and impediments to international trade cannot be other than a slow and arduous process.

Evolved as a temporary program to meet a great emergency, they know that the Farm Bill is at best an imperfect adaptation to the necessities of the immediate situation.

They have faith in the application of intelligence to the facts.

A most important feature of the broad executive powers granted by the administration's domestic legislation is that most of the powers granted are either for a limited period or else are permissive rather than mandatory.

Both the Farm Bill and the National Industrial Recovery Act can likewise be repealed or modified by Congress either in whole or in part, if Congress and the country at large so desire.

With a return to more normal conditions, it is to be hoped that the country will then be more disposed to listen to the argument that, since the symptoms of the breakdown of capitalism are world-wide, capitalism cannot be preserved except by international measures.

The crippling consequences of economic nationalism upon American products and, particularly, American agriculture are too obvious for extended comment.

All over the world nations are trying to make themselves economically self-sufficient, with the result that in each the standard of living of the people is lowered.

While wheat, for instance, as produced on a large scale in Canada, the United States and Argentine, is available in the world markets at a fraction of the price maintained in European countries such as France, Germany and Italy, those countries are paying their farmers large bounties to grow the grain.

While huge stocks of rubber remain unsold in the East Indies and Brazil, experts in other countries vainly seek to discover a domestic source of rubber or its equivalent.

This brings us to the solution which is persuasively indicated in the following statement, although at the risk of over-simplification:

> "In the United States we have a great shortage of finished manufactures in the hands of retailers, jobbers and manufacturers, but we have a glut of raw materials and farm products. In Europe there is a shortage of all three things, low inventories of imported foods and imported raw materials, the result of three and a half years of cruel money market pressure and liquidation. If these two markets can be got together, we have the basis of an almost explosive rise in the price of foods and raw materials on this side of the water and an almost explosive expansion of manufacturing activity on both sides of the water. The producers of foods and raw materials, with rising prices for their products, will buy manufactured goods again, and the factories, expanding their activity and taking on new labor, will generate increased demand for one another's products." [1]

[1] Anderson, *Some Fallacies Underlying the Demand for Inflation,* Chase Economic Bulletin, Vol. XIII, No. 2, p. 18 (May 9, 1933).

CHAPTER VIII

TAXATION AND OTHER MATTERS

THOSE who have analyzed the farm problem will appreciate that it is not a kind of disorder that can be cured by medicine from a single bottle. The reader should not be misled into an erroneous idea that the author believes that any single prescription, such as might be afforded by changes in the field of international policy, will afford a complete cure of agricultural distress.

In the present chapter we shall briefly summarize other matters which need to be included in the regimen in order to restore the patient to health. Most of these matters fall within President Roosevelt's farm relief program.

Taxation. There is probably no political problem in the whole country which transcends in public interest the problem of taxation. The situation is not a pleasant one.

To a large extent the problem is a by-product of industrialization. Except for the major burden of federal taxation which is due to the cost of war and of preparation for war, the enlarged cost of running the federal government is due, to a measurable extent, to the growth of interstate industry and the development of its control beyond the reach of effective state action.

Industrialization necessitates an expansion of governmental powers on a scale utterly foreign to the needs of a purely agricultural community. With the increase of matters requiring interstate or national solutions, it is inevitable, as well as necessary, that the powers of the federal government should be correspondingly expanded. It is indispensable that we should have governmental authority commensurate with the scope of the ills and evils which call for governmental intervention.

Along with the centralizing tendencies of the times, the general public is inclined to over-emphasize the unpopular burden of federal income taxation, in which relatively few farmers, as well as few of the general population, have a direct and immediate interest. This is perhaps due to the influence of the large city newspapers, in which less space has been given to the appalling inequities of state and local taxation than the seriousness of the matter merits.

The farmers' great complaint, in most states, is that land taxes, to all intents and purposes, approach confiscation.

The justice of the farmers' cry was recognized by President Hoover at the Richmond Conference of Governors in 1932, staunch opponent that he ever was of such matters as the equalization-fee, export-debenture and domestic-allotment plans:

> "The tax burden upon real estate is wholly out of proportion to that upon other forms of property and income. There is no farm relief more needed today than tax relief, for I believe that it can be demonstrated that the tax burden upon the farmer today exceeds the burden upon other groups."

With this all authorities will agree, as well as with the reasons given by Mr. Hoover why the times require either the elimination or revision of the general property tax, so that it won't work to the farmer's disadvantage:

"The taxes upon real property are the easiest to enforce and the least flexible of all taxes. The tendency under pressure of need to continue these taxes unchanged in times of depression, despite the decrease in the owner's income, places an undue drag upon that segment of the community in which real estate is the chief property item."

The following statement by Mr. John E. Brown, President of the State Farm Bureau Federation, voices the gravamen of the farmer's complaint in the author's home state:

"The man who is taxed on the basis of his income pays no taxes if he has no income.

"The man who owns stocks and bonds assesses them at their Stock Exchange value as of July 1st. If his stocks and bonds have decreased ninety per cent in value he reduces his assessment ninety per cent. . . . But the farmer can get no such reduction. Though his land has been a liability rather than an asset, losing money year after year for several years, he continues to pay taxes on a basis much nearer the war-time assessment. The payers of income tax and the payers of intangible property tax are assessed and pay taxes on the basis of what their income is or their property actually worth. But the farmer is assessed for more than his property can earn or be sold for. His assessment is not only higher, his rate is also higher. While intangible property pays fifty cents on the $100 valuation, and that to the State only, real estate must pay both State and County totalling from two to four times as much as the intangible rate."

Apart from the immediate need that assessed values be brought in line with actual values, the fundamental need is for a more equal distribution of the tax-burden between farm-owners and other groups. Much can be accomplished in this respect through the reorganization of obsolete state tax laws. Those who have studied the subject know that the increase in farm taxes over the last fifty years is due chiefly to two causes.

The first of these is the cost of improved schools. A few figures are illuminating. In a special article in *The Nation,* of March 16, 1932, George T. Altman traces in an interesting way the beginnings of public education in this country and the remarkable increase in the amount of public moneys devoted to this object. In colonial days public education was the task of church and charity. For the better part of the last century such public tax-supported schools as there were, were most rudimentary. It was not until after 1870 that the "principle of free, non-sectarian, tax-supported education" became generally accepted. In that year the cost of public education in the United States amounted to $1.64 per capita, or 0.94 per cent of the national income. In 1890 it amounted to only $2.22 per capita, and 1.16 instead of 0.94 per cent of the national income. Since 1890 the growth has been continuous. In 1910 the cost had risen to $4.62 per capita, and 1.40 per cent of the national income. Between 1910 and 1928 the development was greater than in the entire previous history of public education. In these eighteen years the national income trebled, but the cost of public education "multiplied five times." "In per capita terms, it rose from $4.62 to $17.30—this without taking into consideration the money spent by the States directly on universities and public schools." [1]

The other great cause for the increase in farm taxes is the amount of public moneys which is lavished on public highways. Concrete highways such as the public demands

[1] Altman, "Our Growing Tax Burden," *The Nation,* March 16, 1932, p. 306.

in a motorized age cost money—often $30,000 to $40,000 a mile for good concrete of only standard width; much more in the case of the roadways with extra lanes for travel. A super-highway, four lanes wide, partially completed between Worcester and Boston, Massachusetts, it is said, will cost $100,000 a mile. Walter Prichard Eaton not long ago investigated the situation in a town of about 6,000 people in Massachusetts. The public records disclosed a condition that is no doubt typical in too many cases. He found that in 1899 (the population of the town was then more than 5,000) a total of $10,100 was spent on town roads; in 1900 only $6,300 and in 1901, due to some new construction, $14,400. As contrasted with these modest expenditures the same town with scarcely any increase in population and with less mileage (because much of the old mileage had been taken over by the state), spent on county roads $80,000 in 1929, $78,000 in 1930 and $57,000 in 1931.

The state of Massachusetts as a whole is better off than many other states. Since 1917 it has financed the construction of state highways almost entirely out of gasoline taxes and license fees, and recently had only $2,000,000 of highway bonds outstanding. Yet Mr. Eaton states in his article, which appeared in the *New York Herald-Tribune* of March 27, 1932, state expenditures for highways rose from a total of $455,819 in 1900 to about $15,000,000 in 1930—an increase of more than 3000 per cent in thirty years. The cause, of course, is the motor-car.

Henry Ford and General Motors have not only made obsolete the little red school-house at the cross-roads and the day laborer "cracking" rock on the old-fashioned turn-pike, but likewise systems of taxation whereby farm-owners are levied upon to pay the cost of marble high schools and motor highways which are used by many people who pay little or nothing for their upkeep or original cost of construction.

Few voters care to do away either with improved schools or good roads. In both cases, however, much can be done in lifting from the farm-owner the inequitable share of the tax burden which now falls upon him, by socializing the cost over a broader base. This is already being done in many states. New York has found it desirable to drop state taxes on real estate altogether. Massachusetts and other states have extensive systems of state roads which are kept up, in a large degree if not entirely, by gasoline taxes and registration fees. Because all property should bear a fair burden of taxation, it is questionable whether the general property tax should be eliminated as a principal source of local taxes. It should, however, and, in many states, is being supplemented by special state taxes. The subjects taxed range all the way from gasoline, chain-stores and public utility services, such as electricity and gas, to general sales-taxes. In the more highly industrialized states, where incomes as well as the costs of government run high, there would seem to be special reasons for increases in state income taxes and inheritance levies to supplement the federal levies.

There is justification for such socialization both in the case of the more expensive high schools and the more important highways. Many of those who receive high salaries in cities received their education in high schools in the country districts. Contrary to popular belief, expensive highways add little to the value of the property along the right-of-way. Too often there is an actual depreciation of the adjacent land values, particularly in vicinities near great cities where public roads and highways have become lined with bill-boards and hot-dog stands vying, in the one case, for the jaded eye and, in the other, for the jaded appetite of the urban motorist.

A report made by Dr. J. Gordon McKay, former Chief of Highway Economics of the United States Bureau of Public Roads, estimates that, of the 23,500,000 motor vehicles registered in the United States in 1927, approximately 5,000,000 were farm-owned vehicles. Dr. McKay states:

> "Traffic on the rural highway system is predominantly that of city-owned passenger cars and motor trucks. On the New Hampshire State Highway System, 6.1 per cent of the use consisted of farm-owned vehicles, whose average trip was 13 miles; in Ohio 12.4 per cent of the traffic, and the average trip was 12 miles; in Pennsylvania 7.1 per cent, and the average trip was 26 miles; and in Vermont, 10.1 per cent, while the average trip was 12 miles. . . .
>
> "Manufactured products constitute the largest percentage of goods hauled on rural highways. Products of agriculture and animals comprised 16.4 per cent of the total net tonnage hauled on rural highways in Connecticut, 18.7 per cent in Cook County, 15.0 per cent in Maine, 14.6 per cent in New Hampshire, 21.9 per cent in Ohio, 19.9 per cent in Pennsylvania, and 17.1 per cent in Vermont.
>
> "Farm trucks comprised only 7.5 per cent of the total loaded motor trucks on the highway system of Cook County, Illinois, 11.9 per cent in Maine, 5.5 per cent in New Hampshire, 12.7 per cent in Ohio, 7.8 per cent in Pennsylvania and 11.1 per cent in Vermont." [2]

It has been estimated that the total cost of the 172,000 miles of interstate highway now laid out in the United

[2] Quoted by Black, *Agricultural Reform in the United States,* pp. 475–476. McGraw-Hill Book Company (1929).

States may easily equal the total capitalization of the railroads of the country.[3] Much of the traffic on state highways falls either in the luxury class or consists of heavy trucks (which account for the worst wear and tear on roads) conveying freight for profit, which could just as well be handled over an existing line of railroad.

In the old days public roads were built almost entirely with the proceeds of the general property tax, the major burden of which, as we have elsewhere shown, falls on real estate. This was entirely proper in the age of dirt roads, before the great popularity of the motor-car, when most of the traffic on roads was that of people in the local community. It is inequitable today. More and more it is becoming generally recognized that just as those who use the railroads have to pay for the benefits received, so those who use the state highways should pay in proportion to the amount of use. The answer is higher gasoline taxes and registration fees, although the sales of automobiles may suffer in consequence. Where these and other forms of special state taxes are insufficient, the most economically satisfactory alternative is higher state income and inheritance levies.

In another direction, also, there is room for much to be accomplished in relieving the situation as to farm taxes, although progress so far has been discouragingly slow. At the present time many states have a system of horse-and-buggy local government in an automobile age. The high cost of local government is due, in some degree, to the fact that local units, admirably suited to conditions as

[3] *Ibid.*, p. 421.

they once existed before country people had motor-cars or telephones, are unsuited to the conditions of today.

Speaking before the Institute of Public Affairs at the University of Virginia in the summer of 1931, the then Governor Roosevelt called attention to the situation in New York State:

> "No citizen of New York can live under less than four Governments, federal, state, county and city. If he lives in a town outside of a village, he is under five layers of government, federal, state, county, town and school. If he lives in an incorporated village, another layer is added. If he lives in a town outside of the village, he may be in fire, water, lighting, sewer and sidewalk districts—in which case there are ten layers of government."

Needless to say, the army of officials required to administer a complicated system of overlapping and, in many cases, non-self-supporting local units is greater than that which would be required for the necessary functionaries working on a full-time basis. In Indiana and other states, where the base of local government is the old-fashioned township—a governmental division about ten miles square within the county—there is agitation for the abolition of townships and the transfer of their functions to the county. In the South, where the township system was never adopted and the counties are smaller, a great deal is heard of the advantages of county consolidations. Nearly every Southern state has so-called pauper counties. The principal obstacles to the rearrangement of boundaries for the elimination of needless units are local politics, the conservatism of the country people and sentimental attachments to old ways. How great are these obstacles may be judged from the fact that up to May, 1933 but two cases of actual consolidation of counties in the South had been reported—one in Tennessee in 1919 and another in Georgia which took effect in January, 1932.

Land Policies. The depression, which has been featured with a great deal of loose talk about over-production in both industry and agriculture, has focused attention upon a curious contradiction in federal policy towards the farm problem. While the Farm Board and Secretary Hyde were holding out restriction of output as a solution of the farmer's ills and telling the growers of export commodities such as wheat, cotton and tobacco, that their salvation lay in crop-reduction, other agencies of the federal government were telling the farmers how to produce more or helping them directly to increase the acreage under cultivation.

Until there is a restoration of foreign buying power sufficient to afford a reasonably satisfactory outlet for our surplus agricultural production, the farmers will be helped by the discontinuance, for the present at least, of land policies which tend to aggravate the crop-surplus problem. Since colonial days the nation has encouraged land settlement and colonization. During the long agricultural depression over most of the last decade, various branches of the government were actively engaged in the reclamation of land for farming purposes. Expansion of the agricultural area has been promoted by encouraging the settlement of cut-over farm lands, by irrigation and drainage projects financed with public moneys. The federal reclamation service goes back to the beginning years of the present century. Since 1902 millions of dollars of the taxpayers' money have been expended on federal reclamation enterprises. While the aggregate production of the reclaimed land is comparatively small, the soundness of the whole policy is being challenged on many sides. Much money has apparently been wasted on enterprises located in marginal or submarginal areas. With one or two possible exceptions all the major federal reclamation projects have been failures as self-liquidating investments.[4]

The problem of the crop-surplus has likewise been aggravated by the activities of the states. Many of the states, particularly those west of the corn belt, continue to have tax-supported immigration officials whose business it is to attract settlers to regions which are being developed faster than either the soil or economic conditions warrant.

Contrasted with land development policies such as these is the policy of the federal government in regard to protected industry and protected labor. As G. S. Wehrwein pointed out in an article in the *Journal of Farm Economics* for January, 1928, the government has actually fostered the decline of competition in certain fields and promoted competition in farming:

> "By the immigration laws and the tariff we help to create an artificial scarcity which results in higher prices for those benefited; in agriculture, public policy creates more farms to compete with the farms already established, adding to, if not creating, an abundance which means low prices to those engaged in farming.
>
> "In fact, we have gone a step farther, we have actually misdirected land utilization by bringing submarginal land into use for agriculture instead of encouraging its use for grazing or forestry."[5]

There is need that the government call a halt in the expenditure of public moneys for the reclamation of

[4] McMillen, *Too Many Farmers*, p. 32. William Morrow & Co. (1929).
[5] Wehrwein, *Journal of Farm Economics*, Jan., 1928, p. 20.

marginal and submarginal lands. There is even more need of a comprehensive land-utilization plan in which federal and state action will be coördinated.

As a necessary preliminary there should be a nation-wide survey of the agricultural potentialities of different regions, such as was outlined by Professor H. R. Tolley to the Conference on Economic Policy for American Agriculture in Chicago in September, 1931, attended by the leading agricultural economists of the nation. Along the same lines was Secretary Hyde's Land Utilization Conference, convened in the following November, which resulted in the formation of an advisory committee of experts and a committee of thirty-three members representing leading farm organizations, the farm press and interested business organizations, organized with the special object of aiding farmers in formulating specific state and federal policies and in getting public support for necessary legislation.

Marginal and submarginal land may be found in practically every state of the Union—on the stony hillsides of New England, throughout the Appalachian region, in the old South with its thousands of acres too eroded or worn-out for the growing of cotton, in the cut-over lumber districts of other parts of the South and the great Northwest, in the Ozarks, in the more arid sections of the Southwest and the plains states, over vast areas of the Rocky Mountain states and in the great Southwest. It is land that is either too rocky, too fatigued, too steep, too poor or too dry to be successfully farmed. Exclusive of waste lands, there are thousands of acres of land of these various types which need to be withdrawn from cultivation. The hard-working, courageous farmers and farm families that till marginal or submarginal lands are able to produce enough to depress prices, without earning more for their toil than a meager and wretched existence. Until there is a decided improvement in economic conditions both here and abroad, those who attempt to farm marginal or submarginal lands for a profit, instead of for subsistence merely, will have a hard time trying to keep away the sheriff. Their operations will continue to be a source of weakness in the whole agricultural picture.

The present is a peculiarly fitting time for the successful launching of a national land-utilization program, due to the reversion to public ownership, through tax delinquencies, of upwards of 100,000,000 acres of deforested and farm land. E. G. Nourse, argues as follows in *The Nation* of April 20, 1932:

"During the agricultural depression millions of acres of land have reverted to government—county, state, or national—through the inability of former owners to pay taxes or perfect homestead entries. . . . Practically all the reverted acres . . . have gone into what the stock market would call 'weak hands.' The government officials of a State with a large submarginal area cannot possibly be counted upon to hold such lands a moment beyond the time when the first sign of reviving agricultural prices tempts unwary settlers to stake their fortunes on a cheap farm. Still more will county officials be eager to get a few dollars per acre in sales price or the payment of arrears in taxes and the prospect of taxpayers for a few years ahead. Furthermore, there is an enormous area of land no less submarginal which will remain in the hands of private holders throughout the depression period but be thrown open to exploitative development at the earliest chance for sale.

"What manufacturer could face the future if his factory stood in the midst of idle plants which would be thrown back into production in competition with him upon such cut throat terms the moment prices got back toward a remunerative basis? Unless we can devise such land policies as will give the body of suitably located and adequately equipped farmers reasonable protection against speculative operations below the margin, the business of agriculture will remain in a demoralised condition for many years in the future."[6]

The nationalization of our land policies is a task in which the coöperation of both the states and the nation will be required. It will take many years to accomplish. The main difficulty for a start along these lines is financial.

Due to the depression, there has been a drastic reduction of public revenues.

Perhaps the processing-tax features of the 1933 farm bill can be used as a means for financing the federal government's part in a planned program of land utilization just as the land-rental features can perhaps afford a method.

Under the direction of Governor Roosevelt, the state of New York showed what part a single state can play in such a program. By a constitutional amendment which was adopted by the voters in 1931, provision was made for the repurchase over an eleven-year period, and reforestation by the state, of over one million acres of land, which is better suited for forests than for agriculture. The state has been re-acquiring land for years and in 1930 owned over one-twelfth of the area of the state.

It was Governor Roosevelt's view that the New York plan, to which an appropriation of twenty million dollars will be devoted, will pay for itself in the long run through the conversion of profitless land into profitable forests and through the saving of public money at present expended on the maintenance of public roads (averaging $100 a mile) and on the upkeep of rural schools (averag-

[6] Nourse, "Can the American Farm Be Saved?" *The Nation,* April 20, 1932, p. 461.

ing $1,400 each a year) in the uneconomical areas, not to speak of private savings through the elimination of expensive telephone and electric transmission lines.

Farm Debt. Credit is both the farmer's boon and bane. Paradoxically, he has suffered in the past both from a deficiency of credit upon reasonable terms, with which to finance his needs, and from an over-supply of credit when it was calculated to do him the most harm. The farmer, and especially he who goes in for the production of one or two special crops, needs bank credit until his livestock or crops can be put on the market. In addition, if he is to keep abreast of the times, a considerable outlay is required for investment in larger acreage and expensive power-machinery.

In the matter of credit, agriculture has never enjoyed the same facilities or easy terms as industry. The farmer has had to pay higher interest rates. Until the entrance extensively of the federal government upon the field of agricultural finance, the farmer was dependent upon an insecure system of small and frequently badly run country banks. Thousands of these banks have collapsed over the last ten years, and as a result the stream of local credit has dried up and disappeared in many farm communities. In these circumstances the only source of credit is the government. The federal government is in the business of financing the farmer to stay.

Farm debt is an evil consequence of too much credit supplied at the wrong time. Peculiarly it is a heritage of the post-war period of alternate inflation and deflation. It is imperative that the matter of existing farm debt be treated realistically and that there be business-like adjustments between the debtors and the creditors.

According to best estimates, the total of farm debt stands in excess of twelve billion dollars, with approximately eight and a half billions represented by farm mortgages.

How the burden of this debt bears down upon the farmers of the United States may be illustrated by comparing it with the payment of German reparations under the Dawes plan. The total annual toll was a little less, but in each instance the charge in the last analysis had to be paid in goods. In order to meet the payments under the Dawes plan, the Germans had to send across the national borders each year, approximately $625,000,000 of iron wares, textiles, chemicals, coal, potash and a profusion of other goods, for which they received in return only paper receipts. In the same way, the American farmers, in order to meet the interest on their debt, have to produce and sell an excess of meat and grain, milk, poultry and vegetables, cotton, tobacco, wool and sugar, before they can be expected to purchase and consume the articles which modern industry has to sell.[7]

The main difference between the Germans and the farmers is that the case of the latter is not complicated by the problem of international transfer. Within the United States, at any rate, the channels of trade between the farm and the city are untrammeled by restrictions on the free shipment of goods.

Contrary to the impression among the uninformed, the greater percentage of American farms, after the most drastic deflation of modern times, are free of mortgage debt. According to a survey prepared under the auspices of the Twentieth Century Fund only 42 per cent of the

[7] *Cf. Economic Essays,* pp. 218–219. The Macmillan Company (1927).

farms of the United States are mortgaged and 60 per cent of the aggregate debt is concentrated in eleven states, in the corn belt and adjoining regions. Despite a billion dollars of farm mortgages in Iowa, which makes the worst showing, more than half the states' farms are free of mortgages. The survey which we have mentioned estimates that only about 16 per cent of the nation's farms are mortgaged in excess of 75 per cent of their value.[8]

This situation is reflected in the varying attitudes of the farmers towards the need for federal relief. The unmortgaged farmers can view the situation with comparative equanimity. They, or their fathers, have seen depressions come and go; and they know that while the foreclosure of a mortgage on a neighbor's farm means a change of ownership, the farm remains and passes into the hands eventually of a more thrifty or prudent operator. Accordingly, they are inclined to view with skepticism most schemes for federal agricultural control. They foresee that if once the principle of federal regulation of production and prices in peace-time is established, it might some day be used to lower farm prices as well as to raise them. In addition, they are accustomed to manage their own affairs and are reluctant to surrender this liberty of action for the incidental benefits which they may derive from untried experiments in economic and social engineering. It was the unmortgaged farmers who in a poll conducted in Missouri, Kansas, Nebraska, Oklahoma, Colorado and Texas, voted substantially against all phases of federal control.[9] It is the unmortgaged farmers, like-

[8] Clark, *The Internal Debts of the United States,* pp. 27–45. The Macmillan Company (1933).
[9] See Special Feature Article by Harlan Miller in *The New York Times,* May 7, 1933.

wise, who, with a certain degree of philosophical detachment, are inclined to regard the latest form of farm legislation with curiosity or open distrust.

For the 16 per cent of mortgage-ridden farmers, on the other hand, it affords a possibility of escape from certain extinction. The latter are disposed to welcome any scheme for price-elevation, even though it may to their better reason appear a delusion of academicians.

Unfortunately for the validity of an arbitrary division of the farmers into those who have not mortgages on their farms and those who have, the heavily mortgaged farms tend to drag down the value of those that are free from mortgage. Every foreclosure forces upon the market land at a distress price with a consequent lowering of values all around.

For this reason the mortgage relief provisions of the 1933 Farm Bill should afford incalculable relief not only to the farmers who are heavily laden with debt, but also to the general farming population. The general aim of these provisions is to reduce fixed charges on indebtedness at lower interest rates, reducing principal and deferring amortization payments for a few years.

A commendable feature of these provisions is that they confer broad discretionary powers on the administrators (the Secretary of Agriculture and the Farm Loan Commissioner), and the method of procedure indicated is the negotiation of individual cases on their merits rather than a categorical approach. In other words, instead of compulsion, inducements are offered to debtor and creditor to arrive at voluntary agreements for debt readjustment.

While a detailed mention of the technical features of

the law cannot be attempted here, it is to be noted that it is designed, among other things, to remedy an intolerable situation which had arisen in connection with existing agricultural credit agencies operating under the *ægis* of the federal government.

During 1932 there was widespread criticism of the unsocial course pursued by the Federal Land Banks and Joint Stock Land Banks. These organizations, while under the general supervision of the Federal Farm Loan Board, and privileged by law to issue tax-free bonds, cared only about saving themselves and making profits for their own private managements and private stockholders, to the grief of the farmers who were unable to meet the payments on their mortgages. With their bonds selling at big discounts from par in the market, they relentlessly foreclosed on farms and dispossessed the owners, in order to obtain funds with which to repurchase and retire the banks' own bonds. The effect was one of playing both ends against the middle, as the banks were thus able to make a profit for themselves while both the bondholders and the farmers lost. The bondholders were out the difference between what they paid and what they received for their bonds. The farmers were deprived of their farms. The policy which was pursued not only was destructive of the interests of the farmers who were thus dispossessed, but it was detrimental to the entire farming community because it forced on the market, for what it would bring, land for which buyers and anything like a fair price could not be had.

The Farm Bill corrects this situation by relieving the pressure on the Federal Land Banks with federal aid.

Along with these provisions are provisions for the orderly liquidation of the Joint Stock Land Banks.

The bill does not attempt to effect the refinancing of the whole of the eight and a half billions of farm mortgages that are outstanding.

It does establish a means of refinancing on a conservative basis two billions of this indebtedness by authorizing the Federal Land Banks to issue during a period of two years bonds to that amount, with interest not to exceed 4 per cent, guaranteed by the United States. The proceeds may be used to purchase qualified first mortgages, or the bonds may be exchanged for first mortgages, at a price not to exceed either the unpaid principal of the mortgage or 50 per cent of the normal value of the land mortgaged, plus 20 per cent of the normal value of permanent improvements, whichever is the smaller amount.

In return for a sacrifice in the interest rate, and in some cases in principal, the holder of the mortgage can get a salable obligation, interest on which is guaranteed by the federal government. The farmer's distress is relieved by the cutting down of his obligation, and he also stays in possession of his farm.

From the standpoint of both, the result sought is wholesome.

A Stable Dollar. Perhaps no group has more to gain than the farmers from a stabilization of the purchasing value of money. Because of characteristics which make farming fundamentally different from other businesses, farmers are in a less strategic position than industry in general, to maintain prices during a general fall in prices. Gains which have accrued during an inflationary period are invariably lost in the succeeding deflation, and the industry, with an expanded agricultural plant, left in a weaker condition than before.

Unfortunately, there are few Newtons, much less an Einstein of economic science, to whom we may turn for guidance. The problem is the most baffling with which the modern world has to deal. The experts differ profoundly among themselves in their theories. There is no one whose word can be accepted as final on the money question. Careful scholars who have illumined the subject with keen analysis admit the difficulties which make a satisfactory solution, without international concert of action, a baffling enigma.

Most authoritative opinion would probably be found in agreement with the position of H. Parker Willis, who in an article, in *The New Republic* of March 11, 1931, on silver, discusses various proposals for the rehabilitation of the value of that metal with the following conclusions:

> "There is no safe or recognized method of price control, nor is one likely in this generation. Avoidance of excess production of all goods, abandonment of artificial pegging, abstinence from bank inflation and, so far as possible, current adaptation of consumption to current production will bring stability sooner than any other method. This is as true of silver as of any other commodity. It is tragic that fluctuations in the value of silver or gold should cause such acute suffering among so many millions of persons; but this is only one of several similar tragedies of the world today, when people are victimized by obscure economic developments which seem, at least for the present, to be entirely beyond control."

Money, needless to say, whether it be gold, silver, platinum, diamonds, the wampum of the American aborigines or the shell currency of the African savages, is merely a yardstick of value. Since the War, the mischievous yardstick has acted as though it were of rubber.

When we speak of stabilizing the value of money, it is necessary to keep in mind that gold (which is a commodity itself) rises and prices fall when gold is scarce; and gold falls and prices rise when gold is plentiful. Silver, or any other alternative to gold which might by law be established as the yardstick, would behave in the same way.

Gold fulfills better than anything else the requirements of a suitable medium of exchange, because over a period of years the rate of world production has been relatively constant. The annual production of gold has matched roughly the increase in world production of other commodities. The total gold stocks of the world are not subject to sudden increases or losses.

In the view of the gold delegation of the League of Nations, perhaps the most authoritative body which has investigated the subject, gold not only affords the "best available monetary mechanism" but "the world's total stock of monetary gold, apart from any considerations as to the distribution among different countries, has at all times in recent years been adequate to support the credit structure legitimately required by world trade, and the rapid decline of prices which began in 1929 cannot be attributed to any deficiency in the gold supply considered in this sense." [10]

Rather many distinguished experts think it due primarily to non-monetary causes, the economic dislocations resulting from the War, the disturbing factor of un-

[10] Report of Gold Delegation, as reported in *The New York Times,* June 9, 1932.

liquidated international indebtedness, the use of tariffs and trade impediments and the effect of speculative excesses.

The truth is that the gold standard will not work when gold alone can freely move across international boundaries.

With the definite departure of the United States from the gold standard, the money question has become of primary importance.

Hardly any responsible person either here or abroad dares forecast the final outcome of the dynamic situation that exists.

Instead of repeating the more obvious and somewhat trite arguments against "inflation" based upon its readily demonstrable perils, it would seem that "going off gold" was resorted to by the administration, after the collapse of the banking structure, in an effort to offset the decline in purchasing power resulting from the tying up of five billions of deposits in closed banks and to arrest the deflationary process by raising the internal price-level. The immediate effect was a sharp rise in the price of commodity prices and stock equities, which did much to thaw out frozen credits and stimulate business activity during the ensuing months.

On the other hand, "inflation" as a way back to permanent prosperity simply will not work.[11]

Past economic experience would seem to indicate that "sound money," that is, money that is redeemable in a fixed unit of value, is the best instrumentality of

[11] *Cf.* Angell, "Exchange Depreciation and National Welfare," *Pro. Acad. of Pol. Sci.* Vol. XV, No. 3, *Tariffs and Trade Barriers* (June, 1933), p. 20.

trade. A fluctuating currency that is not anchored to gold introduces into every business transaction an incalculable element of risk and speculation that operates as a deterrent of legitimate business transactions. While bimetallism might work by international agreement among the main commercial countries, such an agreement would be enormously difficult to obtain.

These are some of the elementary reasons why it is desirable that a fixed measure of exchange value be re-established in the world and that this measure be gold.

The interest of the farmers of the United States in the matter appears most clearly when we consider the effect upon international trade of a welter of fluctuating exchange rates.

Tariffs and trade impediments of various kinds were primarily responsible for the decline in international trade that went on up to the summer of 1931. A still greater cause for the progressive decline since the summer of 1931 has been (to quote Dr. Benjamin M. Anderson, Jr.) "the inadequacy of internationally valid money and, above all, the inability of sterling exchange to stand the heavy volume of transactions and to carry the heavy load of international commodity financing to which the world had grown accustomed." [12]

It is a common fallacy to assume that a falling exchange rate improves a country's position in international trade. While this may be the initial effect, many experts regard the benefits gained as temporary and the advantages illusory.

While the immediate effect of the abandonment of the

[12] Anderson, "Some Fallacies Underlying the Demand for Inflation," *Chase Economic Bulletin,* Vol. XIII, No. 2 (May 9, 1933), p. 13.

gold standard by the United States has been that American exports are cheaper in terms of foreign currencies, such abandonment has rendered more difficult international agreement upon the removal of tariffs and trade impediments,—the primary cause of the blockade of our international trade.

For illustration, an agreement between two or more countries for the reciprocal lowering of tariffs cannot, as a practical matter, be made, except with relation to known rates of foreign exchange.

As a preliminary to the negotiation of bargaining tariff treaties, it would seem highly desirable that the exchange values of the dollar, the pound and the franc, be fixed and maintained at definite ratios by international agreement.

Most orthodox economists would be inclined to agree that reduction of the gold content of the dollar (such as is permitted by the 1933 Farm Bill) is warranted if thereby the way can be made clear for an international settlement, which will provide for the reciprocal lowering of tariffs and other trade impediments. If not, the results are likely to be futile.[13]

So far as stabilization of the purchasing power of the dollar is concerned, a good deal can be said in favor of a "managed currency," utilizing the mechanism of the Federal Reserve system, working in coöperation with the central banks in other leading commercial countries. The Federal Reserve system is the only area of banking in which a conscious control of the total volume of *credit* in the United States *can* be exerted—perhaps the only

[13] See Hazlitt, "Shall We Devalue the Dollar," *The Nation,* April 6, 1932.

area in the existing capitalistic system in which planning in the grand manner is generally acknowledged by competent authorities to be both feasible and desirable.

There is no particular mystery about how the central banks can "manage" prices. Those who believe that prices can be "managed" by central bank policies, believe it can be done by restricting the credit facilities of the central banks when prices are rising, and extending them when prices are falling. In the terms of the business cycle, this is stepping on the booms before they get out of hand and cheapening credit when business begins to flag.

Such a program calls for a more positive policy on the part of our own Federal Reserve system than it has been accustomed to follow. In official quarters the traditional theory has been that speculation should be allowed to take care of itself—the principal duty of the central banking authorities was the prevention of crises. A more positive policy is likely to be successful on the up rather than on the down side of the business cycle. Likewise it is the more difficult to put into practice then. When prices are rising, the tendency of the official mind is to drift along and do nothing, when doing something, if the situation is misjudged, might entail unpopular or disastrous results. Stepping decisively on the brakes likewise requires a high degree of courage to go against the tide of opinion when private bankers and business men are swept along *en masse* by the psychology of the boom.

On the other hand, it is much more difficult to halt the deflationary process with cheap credit after the destructive forces of the deflationary complex are well under way. This was shown in the first half of 1932, when the Reserve authorities purchased nearly one billion of United States Government securities (at a rate unprecedented in the history of the system). Though the effect of pumping this amount of credit into the commercial banking structure was slowed up by its being stopped too soon and by other happenings, it did, undoubtedly, relieve for a time the banking crisis in June, 1932.

Various critics of Federal Reserve policy believe that exaggerated inflations and deflations of the money unit can be avoided by the abandonment on the part of the central banking authorities of the view that the sole objectives of central banking policy are intervention in crises and the preservation of the money standard—the view that in the past has prevailed in high private banking circles.

Needless to say, there are tremendous obstacles in the way of a more positive policy. Disregarding meddling by political or commercial banking interests, the greatest handicap is the inability of central bank authorities to know beforehand just how much effect any particular step will have. No less serious has been the lack of workable criterions with which to determine how much credit is enough.

In the last few years much progress has been made in filling in the gap regarding the latter. For the first time there are now available dependable indices of the volume of domestic and world production of goods from which deductions may be made as to what constitutes a normal rate of expansion. Public opinion remains to be educated as to the dangers of expanding credit too rapidly at a time when such expansion is likely to result in disastrous collapse later on. Such education is essential if the Reserve authorities are to be protected from pressure by political and commercial banking interests to permit credit expansion in a greater degree than the situation calls for.

Abroad, an index of world production compiled by the League of Nations goes back to 1923. An English index has been carried back to 1920. In the United States Mr. Carl Snyder, the statistician of the New York Federal Reserve Bank, has completed an index which has been accepted generally by economists both here and abroad, and which measures statistically the annual volume of production in the United States since 1865. Parallel with this study, Mr. Snyder made a study of the volume of credit in circulation in the United States, year by year, over the same period. From these various indices, it would appear that the normal increase in the volume of production in the United States is about 4 per cent per year; in the rest of the world about 3 per cent. The World War set back, but did not interrupt, this rate of growth. Also it would seem from Mr. Snyder's studies that there is a definite relation between the volume of production, the volume of credit and the general price level.

When the volume of credit in circulation in the United States increased at a faster rate than 4 per cent per annum, there were speculation and high prices; when it fell below, there were depression and a decline in the price level. From this Mr. Snyder has evolved a theory (which should not be taken to represent the official view of his Bank) that it is the duty of the Reserve authorities to regulate the expansion of bank credit (which they can through the twin weapons of the discount rate and open-market policies) so that it will be increased no more and no less than the normal rate of increase of the country's production of goods. In an address before the Academy of Political Science in 1929, Mr. Snyder summarized this viewpoint in the following brief statement:

> "If the highest national good is subserved by maintaining the practical working maximum of production, employment and prosperity, then does it not seem that, in the light of these new measures, this would be best subserved in this country by an increase in bank credit close to the working maximum increase of trade that can be maintained year after year, that is, apparently, under existing conditions, at something like 4 per cent per annum? And we should as carefully guard against expansion materially exceeding this rate as we should jealously maintain this rate."[14]

As to whether this theory, thus tentatively advanced, furnishes either the best, or a practicable, method of stabilizing the purchasing power of the dollar, we shall not undertake to say. Possibly this much-desired result might be accomplished by the adoption of the commodity dollar. We do not know. The problem is one for competent experts, or future trial, to determine. At any rate Mr. Snyder's figures furnish a working hypothesis of the proper rate of credit expansion, where heretofore the authorities, both here and abroad, have had to rely exclusively upon fallible human judgments.

The most informed opinion is not inclined to be dogmatic on the money question or on the general subject of "inflation"; since it is now generally recognized that easy-

[14] Reprinted from Snyder, "Relations of Credit and Trade," *Pro. Acad. of Pol. Sci.*, Vol. XIII, No. 4, *Business, Speculation and Money* (Jan. 1930), p. 31.

money or inflationary policies followed by the Federal Reserve system, which were made possible by our gold importations in the years 1921–1924, played a part in the speculative boom which ended in 1929. When the attempt was made to apply the controls, it was too late. The situation was out of hand.

Coöperative Marketing. The United States during the last decade experienced an extraordinary series of mergers and consolidations in industry. Farm Board subsidies to the coöperatives were not effective in organizing the growers of the major farm staples, cotton, wheat, corn, etc., on a similar national basis.

The reasons largely arise out of the limitations of the coöperative movement as applied to agriculture generally.

Without the ability to coerce non-members so as to restrict production of a particular commodity, the main incentive for farmers of this kind to become affiliated with coöperatives is not a monopoly price, which will raise the price to the consumer. The chief advantage that is realizable is a larger share of the consumer's price.

As far as the producers of the major farm staples are concerned, the very size of the country militates against the success of the coöperative idea. The Food Research Institute of Stanford University, which has made an exhaustive series of studies of the wheat situation, in 1926 expressed the view that probably not more than five cents additional per bushel could be realized by a national coöperative wheat marketing organization. It is interesting to note that among the principal gains to be anticipated from such an organization are the "lowering of farm operating costs, better control of varieties, elimination of submarginal lands and farmers, restriction of out-turn and in other ways making farming more efficient."[15]

The cautious conclusions of Professor J. D. Black, in his *Agricultural Reform in the United States,* are along the same general lines. A partial reference to these has been made in a previous chapter.

The following statement was the view of Joseph S. Davis, before he became Chief Economist of the Federal Farm Board:

> "I do not believe that agricultural coöperation will solve the farmers' difficulties, with or without the aid of government funds. I sympathize with the coöperative movement, but it is a plant that cannot have a healthy growth if it be forced too much. Encouragement, guidance, and indeed a modicum of assistance, the government may wisely give it in moderation, but no more."[16]

Those who favor the organization of the producers of cotton, wheat, corn, etc., in national coöperatives, usually proceed on the assumption that gains can be realized from (1) speculative holding operations or (2) performance by the organization for the farmers of functions heretofore performed by middlemen. Eliminating the first of these possible sources of gain, it is obvious that gains from the second will depend upon the farmers' being able to perform for themselves more directly and more efficiently the functions of the marketing agencies whose functions they seek to displace.

Here the difficulties, needless to say, are enormous.

[15] See review in *The American Economic Review,* Vol. XVII, No. 2, p. 302, of *Wheat Studies,* Vol. II, No. 1–10, Standford University (June, 1927).

[16] Davis, "America's Agricultural Policy," *Harvard Business Rev.* Jan., 1928, p. 148.

As the Business Men's Commission on Agriculture, in its study of the agricultural situation, reported in 1927:

"In contrast to the marketing of many perishable commodities, the existing machinery in the great staples, wheat and cotton, works very efficiently. . . . The widespread belief among farmers that a large wheat or cotton coöperative would enable them to hold their products for better prices is probably erroneous."

The broad considerations which limit the usefulness of the coöperative idea as applied to the major farm staples are stated in this report as follows:

"For products such as fresh milk, which cannot be marketed over a very wide area and where consequently, the producers for any given market are in fairly close contact, an attempt at monopoly might succeed, but for crops subject to world conditions and produced for a central market by great numbers of farmers, the chance is negligible. It is to be hoped that the coöperative movement will not be diverted into barren or anti-social efforts of this nature." [17]

As respects the producers of special products, the case is quite different. Tobacco is a major farm staple, but, because by far the greater part of the entire crop goes into the hands of four or five large manufacturers, it would seem to fall in a class by itself, affording opportunities for collective bargaining which are absent in the case of other major farm staples. In tobacco, as well as in the case of most vegetable, fruit and dairy products, there is also room for economies in grading and handling, which in many instances have insured to the producer a

[17] *The Condition of Agriculture in the United States and Measures for Its Improvement,* pp. 204–205. Published by the National Industrial Conference Board, Inc., and the Chamber of Commerce of the United States (1927).

larger share of the consumer's price than would have been obtainable without the coöperative organization.

The rapid growth of the coöperative movement from its early beginnings among the California fruit-growers has demonstrated that, whatever may be its limitations as applied to the major farm staples, its possibilities as applied to the producers of special products are based on sound and substantial grounds. One of the greatest services has been in widening the market for special products of standard quality.

In the case of the Southern vegetable-grower, the California fruit-raiser and the producer of fresh milk—in general, in the case of all producers of perishable products—coöperatives are able to coördinate the movement of the product to market and to handle the distribution of the product more efficiently than can such agencies as existed before the rise of coöperatives in these fields.

Whatever is sound in the coöperative marketing program inaugurated by the Federal Farm Board should be retained for further development.

With respect to special products, the limits of coöperative marketing are far from being reached.

With respect to the major farm staples, what the farmers most need is not commodity pools, either public or private, but markets.

CHAPTER IX

CONCLUSION

ALTHOUGH as noted at the beginning of this book, the agricultural depression is world-wide in extent, its causes vary in degree and character in the various countries. It has been the author's object to explore its causes and remedies in the United States, with what measure of success the reader must determine.

In an early chapter we endeavored to delineate the changing economic features, uncovering in some degree the anatomy of the existing economic structure of the nation. In the next chapter, a rapid survey was made of the long contest between the farm and the factory, the significant place it has filled in the history of the United States for the last one hundred years, and some of the areas within which there continues a conflict of immediate interest between the opposing economic groups. Succeeding chapters have dealt with the history of the farm problem over the last decade, the reasons why at the present time we are passing through no ordinary crisis, and various matters, such as revision of our tariff, debt and foreign policies, tax reform, better land utilization, debt relief, a stable dollar and the encouragement of coöperative marketing—all of which, in a greater or less degree, constitute primary measures of relief for our farmers.

An attempt has been made to trace the blurred and shadowy lines of distinction between forces purely economic and those purely political. The author has tried faithfully to portray the effects of the broad sweep of the former without falling into the error, so destructive of clear thinking, of regarding the farm problem as a matter solely of either. As in the case of most of our greatest difficulties, the realistic student finds it difficult successfully to separate the constituent economic elements from the political. The pitfalls that have entrapped so many writers upon the farm question, who have dared to disregard the fundamentally different economic characteristics of farming and of industry generally, are matched by the pitfalls into which those have fallen who have dared to ignore the neglected truism, illustrated by the inescapable realities of American history over the last hundred years, that the farm problem, viewed realistically, is a politico-economic matter rather than a matter purely either of economics or of politics.

In one sense the farm problem is a conflict between traditional America, a land of Jeffersonian farmers, artisans and independent small business men, actuated by a frontier individualism, and modern industrialism, which makes possible our great cities, whose population has been recruited largely from the overflowing populations of the Old World and more lately by a continuing trek from the farm communities of our own country of those who have found in laggard agricultural centers an insufficient theater for energies and aspirations peculiarly American. From the latter human reservoir have also sprung many of the barons of the new order who have carried with them into a more complicated environment a professed and unshaken faith in that same ruggedly individualistic frontier philosophy which still animates the interior.

This philosophy has made the nation great. It is the philosophy of pioneer experimentation, of every man for himself, which, in spite of weaknesses which were never more obvious than they are today, is identifiable with the dynamic changes which have occurred in American life.

It is also the philosophy under which the jungle of modern capitalism got its start.

In this book emphasis has been placed upon the very real conflicts of immediate interest between farm and factory.

In various forms there have been conflicts between agriculture and urbanized society since early Roman times. In a number of respects the continuing conflict between these two groups in the United States is unlike any similar conflict that has ever occurred elsewhere in the world. Never before in human history has there existed under a free government so many people tied together by the same language, worshipping the same God and having a common background of legal and ethical standards, yet compelled by the force of regional differences to divide along the lines of sectional self-interest, rather than that of class, creed or color. No European nation, as the Beards have observed, ever had, for example, "gigantic industries battling for the possession of the domestic trade and at the same time a highly specialized branch of agriculture, like cotton-raising, almost solely dependent for its profits upon a wide and attractive market in foreign countries."[1]

Whatever may be the remedies for the agricultural

[1] Chas. A. and Mary Beard, *The Rise of American Civilization,* Vol. I, p. 664. The Macmillan Company (1930 ed.).

depression in other parts of the world, the farm problem in the United States, considered as a national problem, is unique from the farm problem in any other nation.

It is obvious that as between the two groups that modern capitalism tends to breed—an irresponsible aristocracy of wealth and a propertyless urban proletariat—the farmers are representative of the older American middle class that over the years has become increasingly wedged between the two extremes.

In this sense, the crisis in American agriculture is more than a crisis of a particular economic group,—it is a crisis that concerns a civilization.

A healthy agriculture is not only the greatest assurance we can have of the continuance of the capitalistic system; it is the chief assurance of the continuance, without substantial modifications, of our governmental institutions which, as the sociological historian is well aware, were founded by the forefathers, not to remove existing economic inequalities between man and man, but to free interstate trade and foreign commerce from existing restraints in order to promote the welfare of all.

If capitalists were to consider what is to their best interest from a long-range standpoint they would make the well-being of agriculture their special concern. A moment's thought will illustrate why this is so. As contrasted with Russian Communism and Italian Fascism, in both of which the dominant motif is overhead dictation by centralized authority, a distinguishing characteristic of American capitalism and of our governmental institutions under which it has flourished is an emphasis upon private property rights.

At the time the federal Constitution was adopted, "property" meant predominantly investment in land, which not only afforded to the owner a degree of independence, but entailed a sense of responsibility to the community. Both of these attributes, which are so needed in contemporary American life, to give it character and meaning, are in danger of being lost through the specialization and regimentation which excessive industrialization entails.

For a long time there has been a revolution going on in the nature of property ownership. The instinct for land ownership was never weaker than it has been for the last decade. While basically the modern business man is of the same race as the hardy pioneer backwoodsman who subdued the wilderness,—each has the same acquisitive social outlook,—the revolution in the nature of property ownership creates new social problems that it is difficult for the community to solve. One reason why this is so, is pointed out by James Truslow Adams in *The Epic of America*. "The owner of a box full of papers" is [in Mr. Adams' language] "far less hampered in his relations both to his property and to his community than was the large planter or the small farmer of the North and West. His methods of accumulation and the amount of his wealth were much less open to public knowledge and scrutiny. His occupations and daily life, so different from those of either farmer or planter, bred a different set of qualities. The trader who dealt in securities or who turned over real estate quickly in rapidly growing towns had no need of such qualities as made the New England farmer or such a Southern planter as Washington. His personal interests often became disassociated from those of his fellow citizens, and even inimical to them. Human nature, being what it is, he would, consciously or not, tend to view the public interest in the light of his own. . . ."[2]

The Wall Street boom which ended in 1929, was due in part to participation by the public in the speculation on a scale heretofore unknown; it was due in even greater part to the fact the public was encouraged to indulge in the fatal phrensy by those who were presumably in a position to know better.

Farmers are handicapped in working out a solution of their difficulties by the fact that they can depend for guidance upon neither the overlords of business and finance nor upon the radical opinion of the cities and universities, the latter of which, though it seems destined to play a large rôle in American life in the years ahead, has as yet failed to shake the faith of the average man in the fundamental soundness of the American capitalistic order.

While big business is not lacking in men of wide sympathies, foresight and a sense of social responsibility, there is no class charged with an important social function which has been more discredited by the course of events in the last four years. No class was more guilty, during the Coolidge-Hoover stock-market boom, of disseminating more half-truths that would have disgraced an elementary student in economics.

Because the industrialist, who has for years enjoyed special governmental favors, owes a primary responsibility to the intricate commercial interests with which he is identified, there is perhaps no class less qualified by in-

[2] Adams, *The Epic of America, p.* 176. Little, Brown and Company (1931).

stinct and training to express a disinterested view of the broader aspects of current economic problems. There is no class whose public utterances on the farm problem are more futile.

Nor can the farmers rely for an understanding of their problems upon those who, impressed by the anarchistic confusion of a capitalistic civilization, advocate radical alterations in the existing system of private property rights or in established American institutions.

Some of our most enlightened liberals, reflecting the urban or university point of view, are advocating the advantages of national planning to take the place of the existing uncoördinated and acquisitive scheme of things.

While liberals of this type often express the greatest sympathy for the farmers' troubles, very few of the so-called plans realistically face the vital questions: "Who is to do the planning?" "And what is to be the objective of the planners?"

Obviously, it makes a great deal of difference to the farmers whether the execution of the "plan" is to be committed to interests friendly or hostile to agriculture; or whether, for instance, production is to be "planned" for the domestic market or the export as well.

Until questions such as these can be clearly answered,—which they cannot be, because objectives such as these are political questions about which men will always continue to differ,—economic planning, such as is advocated in certain liberal circles, is not a program that is likely either to appeal to or gain the adherence of the farmers generally. The American farmer is individualistic, practically-minded and conservative in his instincts in an extreme degree. He dislikes to have some one else tell him how to run his business. His whole manner of life tends to develop in him physical endurance, self-reliance and the ability to meet situations on his own responsibility.

From the standpoint of agriculture, the farmers' ruin will be complete if the control or planning of production should fall into the hands of the industrialists and the financiers.

One reason the farmer's point of view receives an inadequate hearing is that he is relatively inarticulate as contrasted with the others who present their points of view for the attention of the nation. Too many of our best thinkers are out of touch with the problems, the needs and the viewpoint of those who live on farms.

Professor J. D. Black has developed this idea slightly differently:

> "I have been living in the East for years and reading editorials on agriculture in the New England and New York and Philadelphia papers, editorials frequently manifesting outwardly the very greatest sympathy with the farmer in his problems; but the very language chosen and positions taken actually reveal a city-minded point of view with respect to agriculture. The editorial writers can not help it no matter how hard they try. Even such liberal-minded journals as the *Nation* and the *New Republic* are city-minded in their points of view no matter how hard they try to be otherwise, because they are edited by people living in cities and in constant contact with city people." [8]

There is no profounder human truth that the individual's point of view depends upon influences of which he

[8] Black, "The Problem of Determining an Economic Policy for American Agriculture," in Duddy, *Economic Policy for American Agriculture,* p. 10. Univ. of Chicago Press (1932).

is scarcely aware, economic or professional training, acquired convictions, the stereotyped reactions of the group within which he moves, the pull of the environment within which he lives.

The gulf that separates so many city-minded people from intellectual contact with the farmers is a species of snobbishness on the part of the former arising from the belief that the latter have not a point of view that is entitled to respect.

As Carl C. Taylor has remarked: "Farmers are not dumb animals whose sole importance inheres in their capacities to produce raw goods. They are people. They constitute communities. They build civilizations." [4]

While they may differ as to methods of obtaining what they want, they have a point of view.

This point of view is not usually couched in the language of the economists, but it is a point of view that evidences mature deliberation.

We find it in the plain language of the plain-speaking people who comprised the so-called Farmers' Relief Conference which recently gathered in Washington to present its petition upon the floors of both Houses of Congress:

> "We have seen food destroyed, and everywhere our crops rot on the ground in a marketless country because hungry millions have lost their purchasing power.
>
> "In the face of this social calamity 'farm leaders' and politicians dare to talk of 'surplus'; dare to base legislation on a theory of reduction of acreage that will fit the present starvation markets." [5]

[4] Taylor, "Our Rural Population Debacle," *The American Economic Review,* Vol. XVI, No. 1 (1926), p. 165.

[5] See *Congressional Record* for December 9, 1932, p. 274.

Acreage reduction, which some men in high places recommend as a cure for the farmers' troubles, leaves the farmers cold, when millions of people throughout the world are near to starvation.

What the farmers want, above everything else, is markets.

As the trained economist would express it, "fundamentally the economic problem of American agriculture is the vast volume of farm wealth which is produced annually, and the small quantity of it which remains in the hands of the producers."

To some the position the author has taken in this volume, emphasizing the need of a low-tariff policy as a means of enabling the producers to retain a larger share of the wealth they produce through the stimulation of foreign demand, may seem impracticable and idealistic.

Those who feel inclined to make this criticism should not overlook the new place that the century-old tariff question occupies in America at the present juncture of affairs.

Since the days of Calhoun, when the tariff first became a dominant issue in American politics, the issue has progressed through several distinct phases.

The first phase was before the Civil War when the Southern planters, with whom were allied at first many of the independent farmers of the West, opposed the high tariff which the manufacturing interests of the East and North wanted, because they saw in it a discrimination against their economic welfare.

The second phase saw the opposing economic groups

less clearly aligned. The Civil War sundered definitely the union of the agricultural interests of the South with those of the West. The rise of big business after the War and the resulting growth of the cities opened new domestic markets; and our position as a debtor nation enabled us, in spite of a high tariff, to send to foreign markets annually a steady stream of agricultural exports with which we paid our debts to the Old World. Nevertheless, there were years of acute agricultural distress. The percentage of farmers to the total population of the country steadily declined, although the volume of agricultural production increased by leaps and bounds with the opening up of the virgin soil of the West.

When in 1887 Grover Cleveland startled the country with a ringing message to Congress, the center of emphasis, as well as the balance of population, had definitely shifted. An examination of this document shows the significance of the second phase of the controversy as distinguished from the first. It stressed the view that a high tariff was a discrimination for the benefit of manufacturers upon every consumer in the land. No longer were the lines of battle clearly drawn between the farm and the factory, as they had been in 1830; rather the emphasis was upon the division between the manufacturers and the consumers.

The third phase began with the change in our debtor-creditor relationship during the World War. Since the War, the tariff has become inseparably bound up with our debt policy and broader objectives of our foreign policy.

A significant characteristic of the third phase of the tariff controversy is the present alignment of some of the manufacturers against our great exporting industries (including farming).

Although the farmers are more definitely a minority of the total population than they were in Cleveland's day, there is hope for substantial farm relief through tariff revision, because a frontal attack on the tariff is not only logically demanded by the existing situation of the nation and of the world, but will be welcomed, for the first time, by some of our biggest industries and by the powerful interests that are connected with foreign investment.

Far from being an echo from the tombs of the past, the tariff question, in spite of the Cassandras who hail the death-knell of "internationalism," continues very much alive. It is an inescapable issue, unless the American people are resolved to embrace willingly the blighting consequences of limitation of output to the domestic demand.

As we now know, our inconsistent foreign investment and trade policies since the World War have been a ghastly blunder.

So too have most of the political measures designed for the relief of agriculture.

Tariffs on agricultural products, of which we produce an export surplus, and easy credits have succeeded no better than the stabilization purchases of the Federal Farm Board.

Credit could not sustain a falling price-level, and while at the present time credit is needed in the farm mortgage situation to save wholesale dispossessions, credit does not offer an adequate solution for the farm problem. It is impossible for either the farmers or for the nation to borrow out of the present dilemma. Credit is too much like whiskey. You give a man one drink and he feels better; two, and the outlook is still brighter. If he gets too much he lies down in a stupor.

The depression in agriculture during the last decade was due partly to the long and continuous disparity between the prices of what the farmers sell and the prices of the things they buy. The hardship of the present situation is caused by the fact that during the depression farm prices and other prices declined unevenly.

Except for the radical expedient of currency inflation, the schemes artificially to bring farm prices back in line with other prices revolve directly or indirectly around our tariff, debt and foreign policies.

As the *New York Times* remarks editorially, none of these schemes are entirely satisfactory:

> "The debenture plan would impose a heavy charge upon the general public and tend to stimulate production at a time when already there is a record carry-over of such crops as wheat and cotton. The equalization fee would involve the Government in further efforts to dispose of each year's surplus as it came upon the market. The domestic allotment plan is designed in theory to curtail production by giving every farmer a 'quota' which he must observe, if he wishes to profit from the scheme; but the administrative difficulties inherent in the project are enormous."[6]

While the latter plan is the most economically unobjectionable of the three, and its adoption as an emergency relief measure is perhaps justified pending necessary adjustments in our tariff, debt and foreign policies, it is open to criticism on the score that it will introduce into a price system, that is already suffering from too great

[6] The *New York Times* Editorial, Dec. 1, 1932.

rigidity in some respects, a further element of inelasticity.

From the long range standpoint, the primary way to save the farmers is by a restoration of foreign markets. Only by restoring foreign markets can we avoid a cruel and relentless readjustment of the agricultural structure of the nation to a domestic basis. A prerequisite to affording the farmers a chance to compete in the markets of the world and to a restoration of foreign demand for our products is a lowering of existing tariffs, the settlement of the War Debts, and a foreign policy adapted to world realities and designed to lessen the causes of economic and military warfare.

In fundamental ways the interests of farming and of industry, though conflicting, are interdependent.

As a business matter industry cannot prosper wih a prostrate agriculture.

The following impressive figures show agriculture's place in the national economy:

> "It purchases one-tenth of the manufactured products of the nation, valued at six billion dollars. Half of the industrial workers of the nation depend for employment on materials supplied from the farms of America. It pays indirectly two and a half billion dollars in wages to urban employees. It constitutes one-eighth of the freight tonnage of the railroad systems, one-half of the exports, and one-fifth of the nation's tangible wealth. It pays one-fifth of the total cost of government."[7]

More important is the human side. A nation's greatness depends not upon greatness in material resources, or in the wealth that material resources afford, but upon the greatness of her men and women.

[7] Ostrolenk, *The Surplus Farmer,* pp. 43–44. Harper & Brothers (1932).

The farm not only has supplied the greater share of those who have risen to eminence in the multifarious national activities, but, in an age of social change, it continues the school for the development of human virtues that are needed if our civilization is to endure.

Professor Wilson Gee, in *The Place of Agriculture in American Life,* describes some of these virtues, which in general are characteristic of our agricultural population. Because the farmer is "an individualist" he is unusually independent and self-reliant. His conservatism is a valuable ballast against revolutionary social and political change. Necessity makes him "thrifty" and "frugal."

Not only is there more "democracy" in the country than in the city, but also more "hospitality," less "crime and lawlessness." What the farmers may lack in the sophistications of society, is balanced by the fact that they constitute "the most religious element of our population."

Says Professor Gee:

"Living in the open, under the canopy of the heavens, constantly dealing with the hidden mysteries of life, dependent upon soils and seasons, the farmer is conscious, as is no other class of people, of the ruling hand of a Kind Providence. He witnesses the beauties of the rising sun and finishes his day's work in the afterglow of its setting. He plants the grain of wheat in the earth and watches it through its stages of growth to the harvest. His soul cries out in no indefinite way that there is a God, immanent in the things of nature and therefore in the hearts of men.

"Few deny the potency of the religious motive in life. In fact, one wonders whether any very high achievement can be reached in a nation or an individual that is not keenly sensible of Deity. Living in the city, surrounded by the works of man, shut off from the beauties of nature, one finds it more difficult to be as thoroughly mindful of God in all things as the farmer."

There are probably more people on the farms than in the cities who have, in a basic sort of way, a coördinated philosophy of man's relation to the universe and to his fellow man.

Last, but not least important, in no group is there more respect for "the sacredness of family ties."[8]

For years the nation has deliberately pursued policies, the collective effect of which has been to stimulate the processes of industrialization and urbanization. Because the economic interests of the farm and the factory are conflicting, as well as interdependent, these policies have necessarily benefited industry at the expense of agriculture, producing an unbalanced condition which, coinciding with a great national and world crisis, has rocked the economic structure of the nation.

Primary relief for agriculture would seem to call for measures which it must frankly be admitted may check industrialization and urbanization on the scale on which they have been progressing. This consideration, however, is not a good reason why such measures may not be in the national interest. Over-industrialization makes for increased economic and political instability.

The world disaster is in part due to the fact that, although the War brought a fundamental change in our national interests by transforming us from a debtor to a creditor nation, we have so far disregarded our own longer national interest that we have failed to adapt governmental policies to the economic realities.

Both nationally and internationally the hard lesson is

[8] See Gee, *The Place of Agriculture in American Life,* pp. 10–17. The Macmillan Company (1930).

being enforced that pursuit of profits alone is self-defeating; that the longer self-interest of all involves mutual sacrifice and mutual coöperation. What the United States, as well as the civilized world, needs, is respect for the principle that the other fellow must have a chance.

Industry has disregarded this principle in the United States. Since Pickett and his gray-clad soldiers advanced through the ripening wheat at Gettysburg to waver and fall back outnumbered, the dominant note in America has been the pursuit of profits. The astounding rewards which industry has paid have drawn to the cities and city enterprises those who have sought the easiest road to wealth or power over the affairs of their fellow men. Since the turn of the century all forces have seemed to conspire to stimulate what for want of a better term must be referred to as the urban complex. The farms, though steadily losing in importance in the national economy, have continued to furnish an environment within which has been born and developed the brains and pioneer initiative which have furnished a large share of the dynamics of a business civilization.

As Dr. Bernard aptly remarked in a round-table discussion on agriculture in our national policy at the 1925 annual meeting of the American Economic Association:

". . . the city has come to be the center of manufacturing, of markets, of transportation, and of credits and financing. This last function—the capitalistic or financing function—has quite clearly come to dominate all of the other processes of production and distribution. There seems to be plenty of evidence that manufacturing corporations, railroads, and sometimes even international relations, are operated or controlled largely from the standpoint of maximum profits, rather than of maximum public service. . . . Under such conditions it is neither the producer nor the consumer whose interests are considered primarily by our marketing system, but the financier's."[9]

The World War, which put an end to the so-called Progressive movement in our national life, likewise contributed to the dominance, after the War, of business over all other interests. The era of Harding and Coolidge in the years to come may be mainly significant to the historian as marking the complete ascendancy of big business over politics. It marked likewise the advent into unchallenged sway of Mr. Gerard's list of the sixty real rulers of America.

In after years, it is possible that the hectic money-lust of the glamorous decade, so recently departed that we cannot as yet weigh its import for the future, may be regarded as less significant than the cynical saying that became current in the country at large "you can't convict a million dollars." And as events have demonstrated, events only have been able to convict it of arrogant stupidity. Only the remorseless working of forces which seem beyond the competence of man to control have convinced people generally that they should not accept at their face value the oracular stock-market prognostications, say, of Secretary Mellon, or the economic mouthings, say, of Mr. Schwab. Reluctantly the conviction has taken foothold that because Mr. Ford has benefited mankind by putting together and marketing profitably a cheap automobile he is not for that reason equipped to speak authoritatively about matters he has never studied.

In the last analysis the awful paradox of starvation in the midst of plenty is the result of the self-interest of

[9] Bernard, discussion, "Agriculture in Our National Policy," *The American Economic Review,* Vol. XVI, No. 1 (1926), p. 167.

the industrialists and the financiers having overreached itself. With agriculture and raw producers, who are dependent upon world markets in a state of collapse, a great segment of our population cannot buy the product of industry. The slowing down of industry, in turn, throws vast numbers of those dependent upon industry out of employment, so that they cannot buy food and other farm products.

Encysted like a parasitic growth over the land is a heavy incubus of debt which is an obstacle to the restoration of economic health. Much of this represents investment that was misdirected during the decade of extravagance. Whichever way we turn, it seems inevitable that much of this investment must be written down, which means that the creditor classes must take their losses along with the producers and the consumers. Resistance to the scaling down of fixed charges, to governmental economy, and to the reorganization of inflated capital structures, and the maintenance of prices through restriction of production or control over sources of supply, delay the reopening of the normal channels of trade.

From the agricultural point of view, taxes should come down, a more equitable distribution of the tax burden which now rests too heavily upon real estate is imperative; freight and public utility rates should come down; the peculiar intergovernmental debts which are America's legacy of the War need to be compromised; tariffs need to be lowered; and we need to eliminate the causes of friction with other nations. The danger of world war is a threat to world civilization.

While these objectives may seem vague, they are only so in the sense that most attempted definitions of national policy are platitudinous. Because of the decline of the agricultural population, the farm-minded leaders of the nation face a dilemma, as well as a grave responsibility. Either the objectives of national agricultural policy must be defined in the terms of the longer national interest, or else they cannot be expected permanently to receive the support of the country at large.

Since the War, America has been at a significant parting of the ways. Our post-war policies, in so far as they have been representative of a narrow economic nationalism, have been based on the premise that the United States could prosper regardless of what happened to the rest of the world.

In certain of the industrial and political quarters in which this fallacy prevailed during the past decade, a new half-truth has gained currency; *viz.*, that the national interest will be best subserved by a closed economic system which will immunize the United States from the risks of world competition. While lowering our tariffs, which is urgently required by our changed debtor-creditor relationship with the rest of the world, means the loss of some of the investment that has been misdirected into overgrown industries which cannot stand on their own feet without tariff subsidies, the alternative policy of a closed economic system means the loss not only of a great part of our foreign investments but the radical readjustment of our exporting interests to the consumptive requirements of the domestic market. With agriculture and a large part of our manufacturing enterprises geared to a world market, it means limitation of output in these lines, with a lowered standard of living not only for those engaged in them, but for the people generally.

What the proponents of a closed economic system dare not frankly face and what those whose interest has been enlisted by an immediate concern for maximum profits seem scarcely to recognize is that, even though self-containment may in a large degree be achieved, its achievement means the penalization of industries which are naturally strong, in an endeavor to save investments of capital foolishly made in those naturally weak. Even more, should the effort to keep output and prices within bounds fail, and the use of force become necessary, it means a drift toward the nationalization of land and other forms of capital, the submergence of our democratic institutions in an alien fascism. The story may be a long one, but such is the logical sequence of high tariffs, over-industrialization, a prolonged failure to adapt our policies to our changed debtor-creditor relationship with the rest of the world, and a persistence in economic nationalism.

If the country is to keep an even keel there need to be developed within the country more men who can analyze the whole situation and put it in understandable form for the people who do exercise their minds. The country can't be run on a Wall Street point of view which is concerned with immediate profits and looks only twenty-four hours ahead.

According to the American theory of government, the people in the last analysis determine ultimate questions of policy. The people generally are capable of making wiser decisions than those high in industrial and financial circles give them credit for. An outstanding fact of the post-War years in America has been the failure of leadership.

As James Truslow Adams is quoted as saying in a symposium in *The Forum Magazine* for May, 1932:

"There has been a great deal of talk recently about our 'business leaders' and the part they are playing in our government. I am coming more and more to the conclusion that we have no such things as business leaders. We have big bankers and big steel men, but those men are all working twenty-four hours a day at their particular desks, looking at all the problems of the country from the angle of a Wall Street banker or a president of a steel company or whatever they may be. They are not seeing the business of the country as a whole. They may have their eyes on prosperity, worrying about whether business is going to get better or worse, whether they should enlarge their plants, and so on, but I don't see that they are going to offer us any leadership for the country as a whole." [10]

The influence of the intellectuals is ineffective so far as the masses are concerned because "they never follow either the politician or the business man." The chief hope for leaders is to be found from among the politicians, for as Mr. Adams observes, "the politician, if he is good, will see the problems of the nation as a whole, which your business man cannot."

Because our economic problems are inseparable political ones also, the desperate need of the United States is for politicians with economic training and a brand of statesmanship that represents a blend of the two sciences.

It has been the object of this volume to analyze the farm problem of the United States and to outline the fundamentals of the situation from a national point of view in order to present a summary of primary measures of relief, without confusing the reader by extending the discussion to the farm problems of other countries.

The futility of this attempt is apparent from the de-

[10] "The Future of American Government," *The Forum Magazine*, May, 1932, pp. 290–291.

monstrable dependence of farming in the United States upon a restoration of foreign demand, and the fact that all the leading proposals artificially to raise farm prices in the United States are intimately related to our tariff, debt and foreign policies.

Even as measures for the relief of farmers in the United States need to be considered in relation to the national interest, so does the national self-interest need to be related to the world situation. When they are, we find that, nationally as well as internationally, the adoption of the principle of conduct of letting the other fellow have a chance is not only good business from the long-range viewpoint but an imperative need if all are not to perish together.

Although the limitations of scope which the author has imposed upon himself in this volume permit only a brief reference, the relevance of the outstanding realities of the world situation can scarcely be overlooked.

The fundamental lesson of the post-War years is the economic interdependence of nations, the practical fact that in the sort of world in which we live no nation can expect permanently to prosper without regard for the prosperity of other nations.

The truly alarming aspect of the world crisis has been the circumstance that, as the depression deepened, in most countries economic nationalism became more resurgent.

Although it has been more than fourteen years since the cessation of military hostilities, the nations of the world, economically and politically, are still at war.

The approach to universal bankruptcy, from which we have not yet escaped, is due in no small measure to an exaggerated political isolationism for which America cannot altogether avoid the responsibility, any more than she can avoid assuming in her own self-interest an inevitable duty to play her part in reviving the normal commercial intercourse between nations, known as international trade.

Without a lowering of trade barriers and a more intelligent policy on the part of the creditor nations, the international gold standard, as it was known prior to 1914, cannot exist. Already a system of primitive barter between the nations of Europe has spread extensively, of which an example was furnished close to home in the exchange between Brazil and the United States of 1,275,000 bags of coffee for 25,000,000 bushels of stabilization wheat. This was after Brazil had tried burning its coffee surplus, having found dumping it in the ocean too slow and too expensive. Up to June, 1932, the following nations, among others, had concluded similar agreements for the exchange of products in kind: Germany and Hungary, Austria and Rumania, Bulgaria and Greece, Bulgaria and Switzerland, France and Latvia, Norway and Russia, Poland and Austria, Hungary and Bulgaria, Esthonia and Yugoslavia. In many instances barter agreements are being relied upon as a method of balancing international payments.

Not the least of the bitter fruits of the economic nationalism is the atmosphere of fear and hate which prevails throughout the world. In every nation people are groping in despair for a key that will solve the riddle of ever higher tariffs, unbalanced budgets, and national distrust, which render difficult disarmament, both economic and military.

This situation is discussed in "A Plea for Economic Disarmament" by Raymond Leslie Buell in *The Forum*

Magazine for March, 1931. In Mr. Buell's view, the present difficulty is that there is "a vicious circle from which the nations have not yet been able to extricate themselves." "Until political barriers to trade are removed, nations will live in fear of poverty if not of starvation. It is futile to talk of peace as long as these fears persist. But nations will not abolish political barriers to trade, and thus become economically dependent upon other nations, until the fear of war is banned." [11]

An instance in support of this view is Germany. One reason Germany has had to raise her tariffs progressively was the necessity of maintaining an excess of exports over imports in order to accumulate foreign exchange with which to effect, without disastrous effects upon her currency, payments owed to foreign debtors. Another reason has been the desire for agricultural self-sufficiency in the event of war. In a public statement, Baron von Braun, the German Minister of Agriculture, boasted that as regards wheat, potatoes, meats and fats Germany now produced sufficient quantities to meet her own needs.

A commentary on this is the following observations of the *Deutsche Volkswirt:*

> "Because our economic policy is governed by the idea of producing as much as possible at home, we pay three times the world price for wheat, double the world price for iron, four times the world price for sugar, from five to seven times the world price for fuel, and have relatively the highest unemployment of any country in the world."

Harold Callender (from whose article in the *New York Times* of October 16, 1932 these references are taken) thus comments:

[11] Buell, "Toward Peace or War, A Plea for Economic Disarmament," *The Forum Magazine,* March, 1931, p. 157.

"This is a notable tariff achievement from the point of view of the producers of these commodities, though the consumers are not so happy over it. Why should a nation submit to such sacrifices in order to be able to supply from its own soil the necessaries of life? Baron von Braun gives the answer. 'Nobody in the world,' he asserts, 'can force us to our knees by hunger today, as happened years ago.' An agriculturally self-sufficient Germany could withstand a blockade. The same reasoning would apply to the other tariff-protected and consequently high-priced commodities just mentioned, for a nation at war would need fuel and iron as well as foodstuffs." [12]

The conclusion to which one is driven by these realities is that taken by Mr. Buell in the article already mentioned, who in the following quotation sets forth his hopes and fears, as Research Director of the Foreign Policy Association:

"Our economic interests demand that the United States work for peace.

"The United States is, moreover, the one nation that can break the vicious circle which the world now treads. Our detached geographic position, which has freed us from the fear of attack, our vast financial power, the not yet extinguished idealism of the American people, impose upon the American government a special and unique opportunity to lead the world out of its present wilderness. Enjoying a four-year term, the President of the United States is, constitutionally, in a much better position to initiate constructive action than the prime ministers of the other leading countries, whose tenure often depends upon appeasing an extremist group holding the balance of power.

"In the past we have approached the problem of the world peace from the political angle; we have talked of military disarmament, anti-war pacts, and world courts. All of these things are important, and we must continue to talk of them in the future. Nevertheless the political problems of the world cannot be solved until its economic problems are solved. The

[12] Callendar, "Fiercer Grows the Battle of Tariffs," The *New York Times* Magazine Section, Oct. 16, 1932.

present world depression is due in large part to the vice of economic nationalism—to high tariffs, ship subsidies, monopolistic control over raw materials, export taxes, reparations, inter-allied debts, the World War—policies all caused by governments. It is absurd to state that governments can and should do nothing to remedy the present economic depression when it is governmental policy that is in large part responsible for this depression. What governments have done they must attempt to undo."[13]

It is to these broader ends that a permanent policy for agriculture in the United States needs to be related.

Furthermore, the program for relief should take into account inescapable historical and present-day realities. Though the interests of the farm and factory are interdependent, they are conflicting. Though also the interests of the nation and other nations are interdependent, they are likewise contradictory.

The antithesis between "nationalism" and "internationalism" is a false one, since our most genuinely nationalistic policy would be to salvage our export industries and foreign investments, by allowing foreign countries to buy from us our surplus production and to pay us the principal and interest due us on our loans in the only possible way, by an excess of imports.

In paradoxes lies the elusive truth.

Not so long ago the Governor of the Bank of England, Mr. Montagu Norman, was quoted as saying that he saw "the light at the end of the tunnel, somewhat indistinctly."

More recently there has been a return of confidence in the United States in man's mastery over events. Too

[13] Buell, *op. cit.*, note 11, p. 157.

much credit cannot be given to the energetic and revitalizing leadership of President Roosevelt and to the emergency measures which have been taken to effect the lifting of the national price level.

The very existence of the government, which on last March 4th tottered upon the precipice with the breakdown of the banking system, has been saved; the emergence of America from the more critical stage of her difficulties, on a path of continuity with her past, made possible.

Party lines have been largely obliterated in the universal thrill at the reappearance of leadership attuned to the national need. Assurance has been restored in the effective capacity of government.

Although the President has been granted larger powers than ever before granted a chief executive, other than in time of war, most of the legislation is of a temporary nature and for limited periods.

With the passing of the emergency phase of the national crisis, the United States, as well as the world, continues to be faced with the necessity for the gradual liquidation of the vast problems which are the world's legacy of the War.

Among our domestic problems, for which a permanent policy remains to be defined in terms of the longer national interest, is the farm problem. It is intimately related to the great question whether democratic institutions, founded upon Jeffersonian individualism, can survive in an industrial commonwealth that has evolved out of a Hamiltonian economy.

As in the case of the solution of the latter question, the solution of the farm question is more than the task of any one man, be he Commander-in-Chief, called to duties infinitely difficult, or an inconspicuous private soldier in an army that comprises many millions.

It is the task of these United States.

SELECTED READING LIST

WILEY, C. A., *Agriculture and the Business Cycle Since 1920.* University of Wisconsin (1930).

A study of the behavior of agricultural prices in the United States during the years 1920–1928.

TIMOSHENKO, V. P., *World Agriculture and the Depression.* University of Michigan (1933).

A recent text on the relationships between agriculture and world prosperity, which relegates to second place monetary factors in the world economic crisis.

HANSEN, A. H., *Economic Stabilization in An Unbalanced World.* Harcourt, Brace and Company (1932).

An analysis of the world's present economic instability, much of which the author believes due to "wrong governmental policies and other unfortunate forms of social control."

BEARD, C. A. and M., *The Rise of American Civilization.* The Macmillan Company (1927).

Essential to an understanding of the underlying forces in American history.

BIZZELL, W. B., *The Green Rising.* The Macmillan Company (1926).

An account of agrarian unrest in the United States against the background of similar movements in the past.

BLACK, J. D., *Agricultural Reform in the United States.* McGraw-Hill Book Company (1929).

Professor Black, who in this volume, published prior to the passage of the Agricultural Marketing Act, did pioneering work in the analysis of crop surpluses and predicted that the gains to be anticipated from the holding over of surpluses till later years were questionable, was called to Washington as chief economist for the Federal Farm Board after the latter had gotten into deep water.

SELIGMAN, E. R. A., *The Economics of Farm Relief.* Columbia University Press (1928).

Work by one of our leading economists, undertaken at the instance of John J. Raskob, but withheld from publication until after the turmoil of the political campaign of 1928.

Duddy, E. A., *Economic Policy for American Agriculture.* The University of Chicago Press (1932).

Papers read at the conference at the University of Chicago in September, 1931, participated in by leading agricultural economists.

Moulton, H. G. and Pasvolsky, L. *The War Debts and World Prosperity.* The Brookings Institution (1932).

Perhaps the most authoritative recent study of the subject.

Rogers, J. H., *America Weighs Her Gold.* Yale University Press (1931).

Valuable for its analysis of the intimate relation between our traditional tariff and foreign trade policies, blindly continued in the post-War years, and the gold problem.

Handler, M., *The Federal Anti-Trust Laws, A Symposium.* Commerce Clearing House, Inc. (1932).

The differing viewpoints of leading experts, developed in a series of lectures at Columbia University.

Clark, E., *The Internal Debts of the United States.* The Macmillan Company (1933).

Recent survey under the auspices of the Twentieth Century Fund, which contains interesting figures as to the farm mortgage situation.

Nourse, E. G., *American Agriculture and the European Market.* McGraw-Hill Book Company (1924).

A none too hopeful survey of our chances to regain our pre-War market in Europe for leading farm products.

Ostrolenk, B., *The Surplus Farmer.* Harper & Brothers (1932).

Gee, W., *The Place of Agriculture in American Life.* The Macmillan Company (1930).

Hacker, L. M., *The Farmer is Doomed.* The John Day Company (1933).

No. 28 of the John Day Pamphlets.

Buell, R. L., *Toward Peace or War, A Plea for Economic Disarmament.* The *Forum Magazine* for March, 1931.

Keynes, J. M., *National Self-sufficiency.* The *Yale Review* for Summer, 1933.

Is Internationalism Doomed? Unsigned article in *The Nation* for August 23, 1933.

Three articles of significance, selected at random from contemporary publications, which deal with the problems created by economic nationalism.

INDEX